THE HISTORY OF ENGLAND FOR KIDS

FROM ANGLO-SAXONS TO TUDORS & MODERN TIMES – A FUN-FILLED JOURNEY THROUGH CENTURIES OF ENGLISH HISTORY, KINGS & QUEENS

HISTORY BROUGHT ALIVE

THE HISTORY OF ENGLAND FOR KIDS

© Copyright 2023 - All rights reserved.

Published 2023 by History Brought Alive

The content contained within this book may not be reproduced, duplicated, or transmitted without direct written permission from the author or the publisher.

Under no circumstances will any blame or legal responsibility be held against the publisher, or author, for any damages, reparation, or monetary loss due to the information contained within this book, either directly or indirectly.

LEGAL NOTICE:

This book is copyright protected. It is only for personal use. You cannot amend, distribute, sell, use, quote, or paraphrase any part, or the content within this book, without the consent of the author or publisher.

DISCLAIMER NOTICE:

Please note the information contained within this document is for educational and entertainment purposes only. All effort has been executed to present accurate, up-to-date, reliable, complete information. No warranties of any kind are declared or implied. Readers acknowledge that the author is not engaged in the rendering of legal, financial, medical, or professional advice. The content within this book has been derived from various sources. Please consult a licensed professional before attempting any techniques outlined in this book.

By reading this document, the reader agrees that under no circumstances is the author responsible for any losses, direct or indirect, that are incurred as a result of the use of the information contained within this document, including, but not limited to, errors, omissions, or inaccuracies.

FREE BONUS FROM HBA: EBOOK BUNDLE

Greetings!

First of all, thank you for reading our books. As fellow passionate readers of History and Mythology, we aim to create the very best books for our readers.

Now, we invite you to join our VIP list. As a welcome gift, we offer the History & Mythology Ebook Bundle below for free. Plus you can be the first to receive new books and exclusives! <u>Remember it's 100% free to join.</u>

Simply scan the QR code to join.

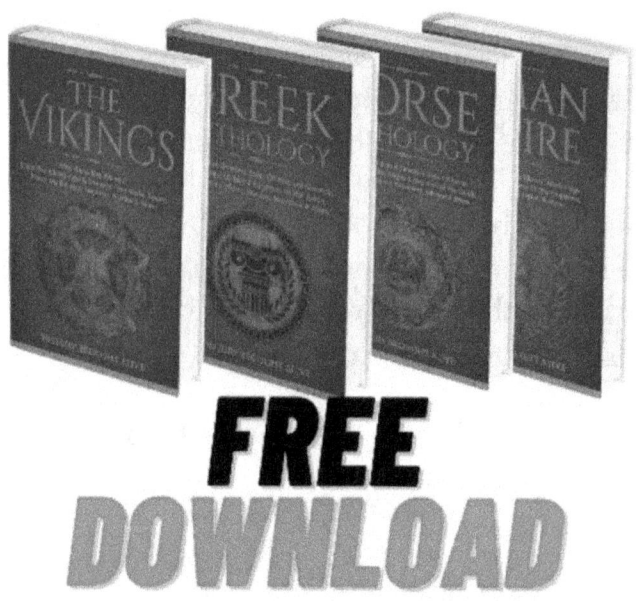

Keep up to date with us on:

YouTube: History Brought Alive

Facebook: History Brought Alive

www.historybroughtalive.com

CONTENTS

INTRODUCTION 1

CHAPTER 1: INTRODUCTION TO THE HISTORY OF ENGLAND 3
- WHAT IS ENGLAND AND WHERE IS IT LOCATED? 3
- WHY IS IT IMPORTANT TO LEARN THE HISTORY OF ENGLAND? 6
- WHAT YOU WILL SEE 7

CHAPTER 2: THE ANGLO-SAXONS 9
- WHO WERE THE ANGLO-SAXONS? 9
- THE FOUNDING OF ENGLAND BY THE ANGLO-SAXONS 11
- FAMOUS ANGLO-SAXON LEADERS AND EVENTS 14
  - *Famous Rulers* *14*
- FUN FACTS ABOUT THE ANGLO-SAXONS 16

CHAPTER 3: THE NORMAN CONQUEST 19
- WHO WERE THE NORMANS AND WHY DID THEY INVADE ENGLAND? 20
- THE BATTLE OF HASTINGS 22
- WILLIAM THE CONQUEROR AND HIS IMPACT IN ENGLISH HISTORY 23
- THE HUNDRED YEARS' WAR 26
- FUN FACTS ABOUT THE NORMANS AND WILLIAM THE CONQUEROR 28

CHPATER 4: THE ENGLISH CIVIL WAR 31
- WHAT WAS THE ENGLISH CIVIL WAR AND WHEN DID IT HAPPEN? 32
- KEY FIGURES AND EVENTS 36
  - *Main Events of the English Civil War* *38*
- THE AFTERMATH AND LEGACY AFTER THE CIVIL WAR 39

CHAPTER 5: THE TUDORS 41
- THE TUDORS IN POWER 42
  - *Henry VIII* *42*

Edward VI *46*
Queen Mary I *47*
Queen Elizabeth I *48*
The Houses of Stuart and Hannover *49*
THE FAMOUS TUDOR MONARCHS 51
TUDOR LIFE AND CULTURE 52
FUN FACTS ABOUT THE TUDORS 54

CHAPTER 6: THE INDUSTRIAL REVOLUTION 57

THE INFLUENTIAL FACTORS 57
THE STEPS OF THE INDUSTRIAL REVOLUTION 59
The Spinning Jenny *61*
FAMOUS INVENTORS AND INNOVATIONS 62
THE IMPACT OF THE INDUSTRIAL REVOLUTION ON SOCIETY AND THE ECONOMY 65

CHAPTER 7: THE BRITISH EMPIRE 71

THE CENTURY OF BRITISH DOMINATION 72
FAMOUS EXPLORERS AND LEADERS OF THE BRITISH EMPIRE 76
THE LEGACY OF THE BRITISH EMPIRE TODAY 80
Colony Influence in Britain *83*

CHAPTER 8: MODERN ENGLAND 85

ENGLAND IN THE 20TH AND 21ST CENTURIES 85
England and World War I *86*
England and World War II *87*
FAMOUS FIGURES AND EVENTS OF MODERN ENGLISH HISTORY .. 89
Figures in Politics *90*
ENGLAND TODAY AND ITS PLACE IN THE WORLD 96

CONCLUSIONS 99

REFERENCES 105

INTRODUCTION

Why was Queen Elizabeth the queen of England? Why are England, Wales, and Scotland referred to as "Britain?" Who were the first inhabitants of the island? Did you know that the Industrial Revolution started in England? These are some of the few questions that your children might have when they are learning about Britain.

However, if you have ever tried to buy a book to learn about the history of England, you might have seen that rare are the times where all the information is in one place. There are books about specific subjects, but there is a lack of material that contains all the historic information in a comprehensive and straight to the point manner in the market.

In addition to this, maybe the books you have found do not have enough pictures for the stories. Perhaps they are more focused on adult content rather than information for children. Maybe they just weren't entertaining enough to hold your children's attention because they simply were not appropriate for the audience.

With this book, you have found a solution that will appeal to children of all ages. With a simple language that will help them develop strong reading skills, this book will allow them to learn about culture, history, and traditions of the British. We have ascertained that the chapters are not too long to ensure that their attention is maintained as they read.

History Brought Alive is composed of a body of experts in history and mythology with over ten published books in the market that have positive ratings on Amazon. The best feature of our books is that they contain all the information in one place, enabling easy study in which your child will learn all about history through fascinating details in an entertaining manner.

In addition to the important moments in Britain's history, we will also provide you with fun facts and amusing details that will certainly entertain your child. After all, learning can also be fun; why not? It is possible to learn about history and align it with fun facts and interesting stories that will peak the child's curiosity and keep their attention focused on the reading.

This book will provide you and your family with all of this—a fun and interesting way to learn about England, all in one book. Therefore, look no more! You have found the best option to teach your children. Are you ready to embark on this adventure? Let's go!

CHAPTER 1
INTRODUCTION TO THE HISTORY OF ENGLAND

What is the first thing that you think about when you hear the name "England?" Maybe the first thought you have is about queens and kings. Well, good for you! That is a great start. In fact, England is known throughout its history until today for its monarchy system, which means that it is ruled by kings and queens. In this book, even though we will most certainly talk about these rulers and why they were important for the country's history, we are also going to see much more.

However, to start off, you might like some context, right? Well, don't you worry about that! We can do that too. In fact, this is what the first chapter of this book is about—telling you the things you need to know that will later help you understand some of the important historic events I will talk about. Without further delay, should we start? Get comfortable wherever you are because this will be a journey that I am sure you will enjoy.

What Is England and Where is it Located?

England is a country located on the continent of Europe. It is part of an island, called "Great Britain," that also has the countries of Wales and Scotland, both of which it borders. In addition to this, and you might recognize what I am about to say next, England is part of the United Kingdom; does that ring a bell? If it does, but you don't quite understand what it is, I'll explain it.

The United Kingdom is a mostly political union that includes England, Scotland and Wales, and another country that is not located on the island of Britain, called "Northern Ireland." Now, you might be asking yourself, *What does it mean that they are politically united? Are they one country?* Well, yes. This is because the queen or king of England is the same for these countries—they have only one government. Therefore, we could say that, based on the official government documents, Great Britain is an "island country."

To understand this, there are three different and important names to remember, and to make it easy for you, I am going to separate them and write them out individually:

- **Great Britain** or **Britain:** The geographical name of the island on which Wales, Scotland, and England are located.
- **England:** The largest individual country on the island of Great Britain and which you will learn about in this book. Its capital is called "London," and it is home to the rulers of the United Kingdom, who carry the labels "queen" or "king."
- **United Kingdom:** The political union of four countries—the three in Great Britain plus Northern Ireland—meaning that they are all reigned by the monarch who is in power.

Now, I mentioned that England is located on the island of

Britain, which means that it is a piece of land that is surrounded by water on all sides. In this case, the country is located to the south of the island and is bordered to the east by the Northern Sea, to the south, by the English Channel and the Celtic Sea to the south, and by the Atlantic Ocean to the west. In addition to this, it also shares its western border with Wales and its northern border with Scotland.

One curious piece of information is that because England is politically a part of the United Kingdom, it technically does not have a capital. However, because of its size, importance, and because it is where the government headquarters are located, London is usually referred to as the country's capital (*Population of England 2021*, n.d.). It has an estimated population of approximately 56 million people, and can you guess what is its largest city? If you said, "London," then you are correct! London is the largest city in both England and in the United Kingdom, with almost 9 million people living in it!

England has its own flag, which is white with a red cross stretching from the top to the bottom of the flag. However, you should not confuse it for the Great Britain flag, which you must have certainly seen already. The flag for Great Britain has a deep blue background with red and white lines that make the form of a cross and of an 'X'. You must have already seen this flag and would immediately recognize it if you saw it (especially because several people use this design as a "fashion" article on decorations and other artifacts).

Fun fact: Did you know that millions of people visit England every year? This is because of some of the famous landmarks that it has, which we will talk about in the last chapter, or because they want to see the huge castles that were built in the country, or just because they feel comfortable speaking the country's official language.

Can you tell me what this language is? Yes! They speak English in England. In fact, if you take a look at the name, you will see it is quite similar. You must think it is because English, England... It makes sense, right? Well, let me be the first to tell you that while many people have the same idea you did, this is, in fact, incorrect. The word "English" comes from a region in Germany and was adopted by England when it was invaded. If you are curious, stay tuned because we will talk about this in the next chapter of this book.

So far, this might not seem very interesting, and you might be thinking *Why do I have to learn about England's history*? There are, in fact, several reasons for this, and I will give them to you right now.

Why Is it Important to Learn the History of England?

The first reason why you should learn the history of England is because the country has been a main character in the development of the world as we know it. For example, did you know that although the United States was discovered by the Spanish navigator Christopher Columbus, its first immigrants were actually English pilgrims who were fleeing persecution in England? I won't get into much detail, but the British were so present and settled so well in the United States that this is the reason why they speak English today.

Another important thing to know about England is that the country was invaded many times throughout its history. First came the Anglo-Saxons, then the Vikings, the Danish, and the Normans. Yes, I know, quite a handful! All of these different invaders played a different role in the development of the country's history to make it what it is today. In addition to this, England was so important that, even when it became a major power, emperors wanted to invade it, like the French general Napoleon Bonaparte.

England was also the place where the Industrial Revolution started, home to the famous playwright of Romeo and Juliet, William Shakespeare, and land of the most known detective of all times, Sherlock Holmes. The importance of the English cannot be overstated, since as time passed, they grew as a nation and became an influential country all over the world. At one point, they even had the greatest navy in the whole world! Everybody feared the English.

But let's not get ahead of ourselves—we will see all of this as you continue reading this book. What I want you to understand is that England has played a very important part in world history in shaping some customs and traditions that we have today. While some of them are more related to politics and economy, others are related to habits that we still carry out today. Don't you think it's cool to know why things are the way they are? Where do your traditions come from? Why are things done a certain way? If you do, then let me tell you; you have come to the right place. I will talk about all of this in this book and do my best to teach you everything there is to know about the most relevant facts in English history.

What You Will See

I bet I have gotten you excited to know what to expect in this book. Well, dear reader, let me tell you; I won't be shy when telling you the information you need to know to become a master in English history. We are going to talk about invasions, wars, and battles. I will tell you who some of the main characters were throughout English history and the important part that they played in making the country what it is today. We will also see queens, kings, and different rulers who came to power throughout time and why they are so important.

But I also want to help you understand where certain things came from, so I will talk about English culture and traditions so you can see how these relate to things we do today. I also want to tell you the great story of why the English have a church of their own, the English Church, and how this came to be. Finally, we will talk about England today and the importance that it has to the world. We will, of course, talk about Queen Elizabeth and King Charles and all of their most important relatives because I bet you are curious about their stories as well.

To start off, we are going back to the beginning—way back indeed—to when England wasn't even a country. Our story starts in the century of 5th CE, when people from the Germanic area traveled west and reached the island that is known today as Britain. Their names? This might sound familiar to you; they were the Anglo-Saxons, and it is with them that our journey begins.

CHAPTER 2
THE ANGLO-SAXONS

A long, long time ago, most of Europe was composed of populations that lived from the land. It was around the same time that the Romans were the most important civilization in the world. They were so big that their reach spread out to what we know as Britain today. However, as the Roman empire started falling, other civilizations started taking power over territories that were, at first, dominated by them. And this is where our story starts; when the Anglo-Saxons left their native land, in what is known today as Germany, Denmark, and Norway, to sail west and conquer British territory.

Who Were the Anglo-Saxons?

Although they were known as the "Anglo-Saxons," they were actually composed of three different tribes in Northern Europe: The Angle, the Saxons, and the Jute. They had tried before to invade the island, but the soldiers from the Roman empire were so powerful that they did not succeed, and this was around 400 CE. However, approximately 50 years later, the Romans started to lose force and they tried again, this time succeeding.

At first, they were very few and they settled in the east of the island, since this was the closer part of the land from where they entered. However, as more people came, they started spreading out and established themselves in different parts of the country, but this does not mean that they all lived happily together. Quite the contrary. Each of these tribes settled in a different place on the island and built their own kingdom, with their own dialects, cultures, and traditions.

The eight kingdoms that were established based on these settlements were:

- Kent, occupied by the Jutes.
- East Anglia, Middle Anglia, Mercia, and Northumbria, occupied by the Angles.
- Sussex, Essex, and Wessex, occupied by the Saxons.

Each had their own rulers and lived independently, but not all was as peaceful as you might imagine. Britain had native people living there, known as the "Celtics," and they tried to battle off these tribes, but were unsuccessful. The native British became scarce, and with time, they began to be integrated with these tribes through marriage and having children.

But I still don't understand why the chosen name was Anglo-Saxons. Well, here is the thing, the Angles and the Saxons tribes were the largest that came to the island, as you might have noticed by the number of kingdoms that each of them established. Because of this, throughout time, they became known as the "Anglo-Saxons." Therefore, it is believed that the Anglo-Saxons are those that are members of these three tribes and of the native people that lived on the island and their consequent offspring.

These kingdoms each had their ruler and were independent of each other—and it started this way for a long time, from 650-800 CE. During this time, most of the island was occupied, and because of their interactions, they started having a similar dialect that today is known as "Old English." They still had their beliefs and customs that they had brought from their native land, but this was about to change in 871 CE, when the first king of a part of what would later be known as the "Kingdom of England" came to power: King Alfred the Great.

The Founding of England by the Anglo-Saxons

The first step toward changing the eight kingdoms into one land happened around 604 CE. Now, you remember when I said that Britain was taken over near the time of the Roman Empire? Well, even though most of it had collapsed, the Christian church was still acting in trying to convert as many people as possible. The Anglo-Saxons were previously pagans and had their own belief system, but approximately in the year of 604 CE, an Italian monk named Augustine was sent to convert the people of the island.

The king of the kingdom of Kent at the time, King Aethelberht, was his focus, but the monk found very little resistance from him because his wife was already a Christian. Kent then became the first English kingdom to fully convert to the new religion, leaving behind its pagan beliefs and adopting the Christian Church. With this, the door was open to receiving missionaries who started coming to the island, which soon adopted Christianity. It was also the pope at the time, Pope Gregory the Great, who first gave England the name that it has today. He referred to the land as "Angle-

Land," which if you read out loud, will sound strikingly similar to England.

Nevertheless, the country still remained divided into seven kingdoms, with the occasional war among them. However, Christianity was thriving in the region and the people were succeeding. This attracted a lot of attention from other civilizations who wanted a part in this success. One of these were the Vikings, who were native of the region that we know today as Scandinavia. In the early 9th century, around the year 820 CE, the Vikings started sailing towards Britain and created havoc among the population. They took over governments and took advantage of the political differences between the kingdoms to entice war and weaken political forces.

And this is exactly where Alfred the Great comes in. He was the son of a previous ruler, and during his reign of the Kingdom of Mercia, saw that the Viking raids were getting stronger and harder to defeat. In one very important battle, he defeated the Danish and, at the same time, was able to convert the Kingdom of East Anglia to Christianity and unite the territories. This was celebrated among the people, since their influence was spreading, and they were taking control over the island, and the resistance built by Alfred was seen as a welcome relief.

At this time, England existed with a division of the kingdoms and with some Danish settlements. However, it was King Alfred's desire to unite all the kingdoms once and for all and build a solid front against other future invasions. However, he was only able to do this partially before he died. However, when his son, Edward, took power, this was about to change. Together with his sister, Aethelflaed, ruler of Mercia, they started to raid the Danish territories in England

and reconquer them. Little by little, they started to gain back the territories that had been taken away from them and expelled the Danish from their land. At last, a union seemed to be close for the Anglo-Saxons.

It finally happened after Edward died and his son, Athelstan took power, in 924 CE. Through marriage, he gained control of the full territory of the country of England, and for once, the whole territory was under the reign of one king. This continued to be true throughout the centuries as time went by, with the occasional war and territory separation, although these were always remedied quite quickly.

Several kings ruled the territory during this time, bringing improvements to the country and trying to bring unified measures that would satisfy the population. One of the main challenges that they faced were the different customs and traditions that the people had, since they were all from different origins. Despite that, the kings historically tried to respect the differences and maintain peace between the people by letting them carry out as usual, even though they did charge high taxes and a percentage of the land as an easy way to ensure that power was maintained.

During this time, the kings that were in power still had to deal with a certain number of internal wars as well as the increase of the influence of Christianity and the church. The Danish were still presented as a threat and even took power in the beginning of the 11th century. However, Danish rule did not last long, as another civilization came and took power by killing Harold Godwinson, the last of the Anglo-Saxon kings in 1066 CE, in an epic battle called the "Battle of Hastings." The Anglo-Saxon period came to an end and gave place to the Normans, which we will learn more about in the next chapter.

Famous Anglo-Saxon Leaders and Events

Now that you have a clear idea of what happened during the existence of the Anglo-Saxons and the creation of what would be known today as England, let's look at a timeline of the events that took place from the arrival of the three tribes until the Normans took power in 1066. In this section, I am going to give you bullet points with the information so that you can follow the information better and identify the specific historic events that took place at each time. Are you ready?

- **410 CE:** The Romans leave Britain after the collapse of the empire.
- **449-450 CE:** Arrival of the first tribes to Britain and the expelling of the remaining Romans from the Island.
- **Around 455-627 CE:** Establishment of the eight kingdoms throughout the territory that would later become known as England.
- **Around 597-601 CE:** Arrival of Augustine and conversion of the king of Kent to Christianity.
- **Around 787 CE:** Beginning of the Viking invasions.
- **Around 850 CE:** The eight kingdoms became unified in three different territories: Northumbria, Mercia, and Wessex.
- **Around 924 CE:** Unification of England.
- **1016-1042 CE:** England is ruled by the Danish, and the first leader is King Cnut.
- **1066 CE:** Battle of Hastings and the Norman conquest by William the Conqueror.

Famous Rulers

Let's take a closer look at the most famous Anglo-Saxon

leaders and the impact they had in history.

- **King Alfred, the Great (reign from 871-899):** The most important achievement of the reign of King Alfred was the strengthening of the Anglo-Saxon army. He built a powerful navy that was able to defend the country from invasions and fight off raiders. Because of this, he was able to avoid more Viking invasions of England and reached a peace treaty with them in 886. With the peace treaty, he expanded the reach of the Wessex kingdom which would later become England. Other achievements included the translation of books that he considered important and the establishment of laws to the existing code.
- **King Edward (reign from 899-924):** Was Alfred the Great's son and took the first step into the unification of England when he married the ruler of Mercia and ruled both the kingdoms of Mercia and Wessex.
- **King Athelstan (reign from 924-939):** Son of King Edward, he became the first ruler of a unified England after expanding his territory into the kingdom of Kent, the last one that remained outside of his rule. He was known for creating laws and taxing the countries of Wales and Scotland, who also conceded and fell under his reign. He left no heirs to the throne.
- **King Cnut (or Canute), the Great (reign 1016-1035):** Became the first King of England under Danish rule after marrying the previous king's widow. At the same time that he was the king of England, he was also the king of Denmark and Norway, making it possible to have all three countries collaborate and start strategic alliances. However, despite ruling over all three countries, he was unable to maintain a unified England

because of the disputes that arose in the country because of his political policies and religion.
- **King Harold II (reign 1066):** After the reign of King Cnut, a few other kings took power and maintained peace and a good relationship with other nations. However, during the reign of King Harold, in 1066, the Normans, who had been pressuring to take over power, finally succeeded, claiming that the king did not have royal blood. He was killed in 1066 during the most famous battle of the period, the Battle of Hastings, led by William, the duke of Normandy, and England surrendered to Norman power for almost 100 years.

Fun Facts About the Anglo-Saxons

- Did you know that still today there are certain regions of England that still are referred to with the names they had as an Anglo-Saxon Kingdom? This is the case with Sussex, Essex, Wessex, and Kent.
- In addition to having these regions in the country, some nobles have titles that refer to these regions, such as the duke of Kent, Countess of Wessex, and the earl of Essex.
- Have you ever heard about King Arthur? If you have, you might be interested to know that it is believed that he existed during the period of the Anglo-Saxon invasion of Britain. According to the legend, he was a Britain native who fought the Saxons during their occupation and was famous for having the knight fellowship of the Round Table.
- A lot of the English that we know today, came from the Anglo-Saxon period. One example of this are the names of the days of the week, which used to have a similar structure and sound to what we have today.

- Many of the people who came from continental Europe to Britain were farmers looking for better land to grow food or mercenaries. Even though they had complete cities that were previously built by the Romans, they tore everything down and started their own constructions according to the architecture they knew.
- What you see in movies from medieval times portray almost exactly what the traditions of the Anglo-Saxons were like. They ate a lot of bread and drank beer, all which came from the wheat they planted, much like they are portrayed on television.
- The famous *Beowulf* poem about a warrior came from the Anglo-Saxon period.
- The Anglo-Saxons used clothes that were made from natural woven fibers. Some of the pieces they used included tunics, dresses, and trousers.
- The Anglo-Saxons had several laws, some of which even gave some rights to women. The law was periodically modified to ensure that it was up to date with the changes in the Anglo-Saxon society.
- The British Museum in London has the largest collection of Anglo-Saxon objects in the world, which include pottery, clothes, jewelry, and ship parts, among others.

CHAPTER 3
THE NORMAN CONQUEST

You know that the Normans took control over England, but you might be wondering how that came to be. Well, this all started after the last "original" king of the Anglo-Saxons, King Edward the Confessor, died. This was just before King Harold II took over the power, and the problem all started because King Edward did not have any children to inherit the throne. There was also his lack of political ability. He was known to make promises to many people, including, as you might imagine, that he would leave the throne to them in exchange for favors.

When he died in 1066, a council of men placed the man who was to become King Harold on the throne because they claimed that this is what King Edward wanted. As you might imagine, the Normans were not happy about it. More specifically, this made a Norman duke with the name of William very angry, since he claimed that King Edward had promised the throne to him years earlier when he finally passed away. This led to a final battle, which is known as the "Battle of Hastings," where King Harold was killed in action, and the duke of Normandy, William, became King William the Conqueror.

I know that you are probably interested in this story now. Family feuds, a fight for the crown, and a battle. Sounds interesting, right? That is because it really is. This period is also important because of the consequences that it brough for England. As you will see, from architecture, to the church, to the language, many things changed or gained new meaning, all due to the influence of the Normans. To understand this better, let's take a closer look into who the Normans were and why they invaded England.

Who Were the Normans and Why Did They Invade England?

If you go to the North of France today, you will likely visit an area called "Normandy." This region was founded by Viking rebels who traveled to the region in the 8th and 9th centuries. As you already know, the Vikings mainly came from the countries we know today as Denmark, Norway, and Iceland, and if you look at a current map, you will see that these countries are relatively close to France. This made it easy for them to reach the region by ship and establish their communities in the new land.

Since these people were now in France, they absorbed some of their customs, traditions, and even the language, adapting their dialects to French. They lived in a similar manner to other civilizations at the time: They changed their religion to Christianity, had a hierarchical system, and were constantly involved in wars and battles for conquering new territory in continental Europe. One of the characteristics of this time is that everyone wanted to be a noble—named duke, count, earl—and this led the region to many political fights, but nothing that would severely impact their occupation process.

But if they were doing so well in France, why did they invade England? As I mentioned earlier, it was a sort of "family business." This is because Duke William thought he was the rightful heir to the throne, not King Harold. The thing is, a sister of Duke William's grandfather married into royalty, but her children, or the duke's cousins, resigned to the throne. Another one accepted it, and he was... You guessed it! King Edward the Confessor.

Because King Edward did not have any children with his wife, he started a close relationship with the duke, his cousin, to whom he promised that he would give up the throne. This had Duke William thinking about taking power someday, but this day never happened. He fought battles, made agreements, and worked on his knighthood and diplomacy, all with the intention of getting prepared to become king. To make matters worse, once King Edward was determined to have William as the next king of England, he sent his brother-in-law to speak to him and communicate that he was to be the next king.

But you will never guess who this person was. If you guessed the future king-to-be, Harold, you are correct! He knew that King Edward had promised the throne to the then leader of the Normans and even agreed to it after Edwards saved him from being captured. Therefore, as a show of commitment, Harold promised that he would support the duke as the new king of England once his cousin passed away, but this did not happen—not at all.

Once King Edward died, his brother-in-law was placed in the throne as king, without even taking into consideration the promise he had made to the then Duke William and to the information that the previous had given him. Because of the deceit, Duke William was outraged and decided to invade England to take over the throne that was rightfully his, by blood relationship and by promise. He spoke to several important figures of the time, including the Pope and the nobles of his government, all of which gave him their approval to move on with the invasion.

After much preparation, in August 1066, the duke set sail from Normandy to England with the objective of taking power. Thousands of men and hundreds of boats joined him in his quest, and in September, they finally invaded England. Although there were a few battles that happened along the coast, the final encounter between the two armies—William's and Harold's—took place in October 1066, in what became known as the "Battle of Hastings."

The Battle of Hastings

The Battle of Hastings was one of the most important in English history. *Why?* Because it determined the new paths that the country was to follow and brought to the country a new king. You remember when I said that King Harold was crowned after the death of King Edward correct? The thing is, while the duke of Normandy was preparing to attack and control the country, King Harold was facing several problems inside his territory.

He was having trouble with other invaders in the country who saw the new political power as a point of weakness and an opportunity to conquer England. Because of this, King Harold's army was constantly in battle, fighting off invaders— sometimes alone and sometimes with help. The king was considered to have such a vulnerable kingdom that even his brother, who was in exile, tried to invade the country but had no success. Because of the constant battles, his army started to decrease in size to the point where he had to recruit peasants without any training to fight to protect the territory.

When the duke of Normandy arrived, in September 1066, the army was already tired, debilitated, and weak, and the king decided to let the peasants go. They had already lost many men in the previous battles and were fragilized because of it. When the king heard that the duke was planning to invade, rather than prepare them for battle, he decided that they would retreat and adopt a defensive position, waiting for Normandy's attack.

Duke William of Normandy invaded England from the south and marched inland toward Hastings. There, he stopped to organize the troops and prepare for the battle that would determine English history. It was there that he met King Harold's tired army, and the battle took place—for one day. Yes! You read it right. Even though the Battle of Hastings is one of the most significant in the history of England, it lasted only one day and ended with King Harold being killed. Although there are different accounts of how he died, the most accepted version according to the stories told of the time was that he died of an arrow to the eye.

After the king's death, the Englishmen, tired and reluctant to keep fighting, accepted the Duke of Normandy as their king. He then became William the Conqueror, who ruled from 1066 CE to 1087 CE. He was crowned in the famous church that exists still today, Westminster Abbey, in London, even though it still took him some time for the power to be consolidated. Despite this, the conquest brought new changes to England, even though he had promised to maintain the customs and laws that already existed in the country.

William the Conqueror and His Impact in English History

William the Conqueror, as you have seen, was raised in France and lived most of his life there, which means that he had very little exposure to English. Therefore, when he was crowned king, although the official language of England did not change, many of the courts and political discussions were carried out in French; the language that he knew. The changes were so significant that, in 1070, the official language of England became Latin, and English was only recovered somewhere around the 13th century. This led to the Anglo-Saxons to absorb several words to their language and help shape what is known today as modern English.

In addition to this, once King William took power, he removed all those who opposed him or who he did not consider friends and replaced them with people of his trust, thus centralizing the power and the wealth of the country even more. This also means that the people who took positions in office and in the elite level of the country were also French. The first step in replacing the former Anglo-Saxons with the Franco-Normans in the English society was then given.

When this change occurred, one of the most relevant aspects of the change was that the Anglo-Saxons had their properties taken away from them, and the land ownership was redistributed among the Normans. This process of ownership was registered in what became known as the *Domesday Book*, where all the transactions would be registered. This process of removing the land from the Anglo-Saxons to the Normans is considered by historians to be the beginning of feudalism, a concept in which there was a land owner and vassals to work on it.

Another drastic change carried out by the new king was made in the structure of the church. Headquarters were moved to larger cities, and several of the clergy that were previously Anglo-Saxon were replaced by Norman ones. In addition to this, several new monasteries and churches were built, and although they were owned by the church, the English church was under the power of King William, who tried to maintain a good relationship with the two popes of his time.

Speaking of constructions, one of the things that you might know about England is that it is a land of many castles. Well, let me tell you that many of these were built exactly during the reign of King William. What is more, not only did the king build new structures where there were none, but he also demolished the existing ones to build bigger and better ones to show his power and wealth.

On the other hand, there was a positive law that he created, and it did not involve building anything—it was the establishment of Royal forests that would be protected and could only be used for sportive hunting. Other changes included the creation of new laws and the establishment of a reformed justice system, higher taxation for the people to maintain the government wealth, increase in the trade between England and other countries in the southern European continent, especially France, and the elimination of slavery from the country.

Finally, King William had to deal with several internal battles, some of which led to bloody deaths and devastation of the land. This severely impacted the country, especially in the north, and it took them centuries to recover from the damage. Because of these internal political divergences, he would navigate between his kingdom of Normandy and England, where he left two consorts to rule when he was away. This, together with all the nobility that has taken their place in the English courts, strengthened the relationship with the French in a cooperation that lasted until the Hundred Years' War, which we will read more about now.

The Hundred Years' War

You know that because William the Conqueror was the French ruler of Normandy and took over the throne in England, there were very close ties between the rulers of both countries. Essentially speaking, he was a ruler in England but also subject to the rule of the French king. As time went by, the next rulers of England became highly uncomfortable with this situation, but it was nevertheless overcome with diplomatic action from both sides. France was, at this time, in the 12th century, a very powerful and rich country with great power over many territories—including England.

The conflict started to get worse when the English wanted to own their own land without needing to be subject to France, and the French were against it. There were two big breaking points that eventually led to the war between both countries. This first was the ownership of the Duchy of Guyenne, who the English claimed belonged to them, but it was still considered to be under French rule, something that England disliked. The second was that, when the king of France, Charles IV, died, a British king claimed the crown of the country, saying that they were the natural heir because of the family connection since the former king did not have any heirs.

The French, of course, did not like this at all, and the war ensued in 1337 when Prince Philip VI of France, King Charles' cousin, and King Edward III of England, King Charles' nephew, fought for the right to the crown and disputed territorial rights. Even though the French army was richer and had more soldiers, the English were better organized, and this led them to win the first few battles in the French territory. To make matters worse, the French crown took away all of the

English land in their territory and claimed that it now belonged to France, and they also interrupted product supply to the island.

The English were obviously not happy about it and decided to attack the French navy. Finally, in 1346, King Edward III, the English king, decided to invade France in a battle that they eventually won. Because most of the English land within the French territory was located to the southwest of the country, this is where the main battles were held. In 1347, there was a brief interruption in the war because of the Black Death, a disease that killed almost 50% of the European population, but as soon as the countries recovered, the war began once more.

Now, you have to think that this was a war that lasted 116 years, interrupted by brief periods of peace, and this made the war favor each country at a certain period of time. There were times when the English had the advantage—they even took over Paris—and there were times that France was winning more battles. The power shifted constantly and lasted during the reign of five different generations of rulers. It only ended in 1453 after the French finally won the war.

The results of the war that lasted so long were devastating for both countries. While the French had lost a great part of its nobility who were killed in the battles and the ones that remained were fighting for power, making its major problem political, in England the situation was somewhat different. There, they suffered extreme economic problems because of all the investment that was put into the army to attack the French—one of the effects of turning many into nobles so they could be taxed and fund the war.

But England's problems were just starting. The population was unsettled, and they wanted changes. The leadership of the king was questioned, as well as the several taxes that they had to pay. The country faced hunger and poverty while the monarchs kept the money from themselves. They had lost all their territories overseas to the French. As you will see in the next chapter, this led to the English Civil War, also known as the "War of the Roses," that arose from the sense of identification of the English and the desire to change the country's paths.

Fun Facts About the Normans and William the Conqueror

- To tell the story of the Battle of Hastings, a huge tapestry named the Bayeux Tapestry was woven in wool and linen. It has a length of 230 feet and is considered a masterpiece from the time. The tapestry has 58 panels that tell the story of how the battle happened, as well as other events, and can be seen today in the Museum of Bayeux, in France. The tapestry is considered by UNESCO a Patrimony of the World.
- This might seem weird, but during King William's funeral, his body exploded because the coffin was too small to fit him, and when they forced it, it blew up.
- William the Conqueror is the origin of one of the most popular names in England "William."
- King William was crowned on Christmas day of 1066.
- Although it is called the "Battle of Hastings," the battle did not take place in Hasting, but rather in an area nearby.
- The duke of Normandy invaded England with 7000 men and more than 600 ships.
- Although he was known as "William the Conqueror," he began his life known as "William the Bastard."

- King William had 10 children in total: Four sons and six daughters.
- Even though he became the king of England, he was also still the ruler of Normandy. For this reason, when he died in 1087, he was buried in Normandy, France, not in England.

The famous Tower of London was commissioned to be built by William the Conqueror and has served several purposes over time: Prison, fortress, royal palace, zoo, and finally, to hold the Crown jewels, an activity that it still has today.

CHPATER 4
THE ENGLISH CIVIL WAR

As you have seen in the previous chapter, the English Civil War ensued in England a little after the end of the Hundred Years' war. While the latter ended in 1453, the civil war began just two years later, in 1455, and lasted for 30 years. Speaking generally, although we will see it in more detail in this chapter, this war was the fight between two houses, the House of Lancaster and the House of York, for the ascension to the throne of England. Some people also refer to the civil war as the 'War of the Roses', in reference to the badges that each of the soldiers from each house wore: The red rose for the Lancasters, and the white rose for the Yorks.

To start off, let's remember what the situation of England was when this war started. The country had just left a century-long war with France for power and was economically devastated. The nobility was not convinced of the rule of King Henry VI and were dissatisfied with the way the country was governed. It also did not help that he was married to a French princess, making the English even more discontent with their ruler.

It is important to consider that the Hundred Years' War was devastating for the country and for the king's power, since a strong parliament arose as one of its consequences. This weakened the power of the king and gave more power to the nobles who were asking for more action to be taken, since they were unhappy with the way office and influence positions were being given out to those outside the elite. To aggravate the situation, King Henry suffered from some insanity periods and had debilitating health issues and could not control the will of his king.

Once the situation was out of control, the Lancasters from King Henry's side, and the Yorks, direct descendants of Edward III, started recruiting soldiers to fight. On May 22, 1455, the first battle happened, and the war was officially declared between both houses. In this chapter, you are going to read all about the English Civil War and its impacts on England, which remain today.

Read on to learn more about this period and the rulers involved, so pay close attention! Lastly, keep your eye open to the final section of the chapter, in which you will learn about the impact of this war on modern-day England.

What Was the English Civil War and When Did it Happen?

Since Edward II's death in 1399, the house of Lancaster claimed that they were the rightful owners to the throne because they were directly related to the former king by blood relationship. Because of this, the house maintained control of the country throughout the Hundred Years' War and until the beginning of the 15th century. However, once the war was over and King Henry VI took power, most of the people were not enthusiastic about it. In addition to this, there was no shortage of relatives to the king willing to take over power from him, as well as nobles who were dissatisfied with the country's political status.

As I mentioned earlier, it was not helped that the king's wife, the French princess, Margaret of Anjou, was obsessed with wealth and power. Most of the time, she made decisions for the king and was eager to assume control. The excessive taxes, corruption, and abuse of power led to the people of York to write the king a letter with demands for improvements of the people's lives. Henry, as a weak ruler that lacked interest in the country's affairs, did not pay attention, and in addition to this, lost much of his influence with France, and the situation with the other Europeans deteriorated even more.

This made Richard, the duke of York who was exiled in Ireland, come back to England in 1452. He was one of the men who were seen as potential contenders to take over the throne since he was the great-grandson of Edward III. It was believed by King Henry that he was the one that started the rebellion of the Yorks because he wanted to take control of the country—and this is where all the problems started. Although that initially was not his intention, the duke of York made it his mission to remove the corrupt officials that advised King Henry VI, but the king soon fell ill and was unable to rule.

To make matters worse, during this period, King Henry had a son who was considered to be the heir to the throne. The duke of York saw his power decrease and was taken to be held as a prisoner in the Tower of London. One of the main problems was that he was vocal against the queen and her advisors. Therefore, even with his role as Protector of the Realm, he was imprisoned. However, King Henry VI got better, and when he discovered what was going on, he released the duke of York from the Tower of London under the condition that he left. His services were no longer necessary, as he was able to rule again.

As a countermeasure, the duke of York decided that he would arm himself and march against the king to protect himself, since he was now seen as a threat. This led to the first battle of the war in Saint Albans, which took place in May of 1455. The Yorks came out of the battle as winners, and this seemed to bring some peace—at least for the next four years—although there was still a lot of doubt and uneasiness.

The queen, still unhappy about the duke's attempt to control her, was secretly planning to attack. This led the duke of York to once again enter battle in 1459, where the House of York won the first battle and lost the second. As a result, King Henry ordered that all those who rebelled against him be killed (supported by the court), and the duke ran away back to Ireland, but this did not even remotely stop them. The war was just beginning.

In France, one of the duke's commanders, Richard Neville, the earl of Warwick, joined the York forces again in 1460 and went to England to fight the Lancasters. They won the battle, and when Richard, the duke of York, was about to claim the throne, he was given succession rights upon the death of King Henry. This was agreed by the Parliament and was called the "Act of Accord."

As you might imagine, Queen Margaret was not at all happy that her son would not rise to the throne and that she would lose her power. In an attempt to take over control, she assembled an army to fight the Yorks and settle the discussion once and for all. However, this time, the duke of York was unsuccessful—he was captured, killed, and exposed as a fake king. While the queen believed that this would be the end of the succession battle, she was wrong.

This is because the duke's son, Edward, Earl of March, took over the throne left by his father and continued to fight off the Yorks. This happened because even though he was also in battle, he arrived in London before Queen Margaret and was proclaimed king in 1461 as King Edward IV. He then used his power to fight off the remainder of the Lancaster army in some of the most violent battles of the war and won. As a result, the queen, former King Henry, and their son ran away to Scotland, seeking protection from being captured and killed.

Once again, if you have developed the correct idea about the queen, you will likely conclude that she was very angry at this outcome and decided that she would do anything in her power to give her husband back control. With the help of the French, she did just that in 1470. Edward IV ran off but remained hidden, where he was assembling a new army to fight off the Lancasters. In two significant battles, the Yorks once again won, but with a greater impact. Henry's and Margaret's son was killed, the couple imprisoned, and Edward IV was given back the throne.

All seems well when it ends well, right? Not Exactly. Although King Edward IV remained in power until his death, when his son, Edward V, came to power, there were problems again. This is because his uncle, King Edward IV's brother, Richard III, who was named as Edward's legal protector, locked the future king and his brother in prison. They were declared illegitimate heirs to the throne by Richard, taken to the Tower of London, and Richard III was crowned king in 1483. What Richard III did not expect was that his nephews would be murdered, and the people would turn against him.

This was when a Lancaster, Henry Tudor, decided to claim his right to the throne. With the help of the aristocracy, and surprisingly, France, once again, England was overtaken by war. In the Battle of Bosworth in 1485, both the king and the claimer fought, and it ended with the death of Richard III. Henry was then declared the king of England under the name of Henry VII.

To ensure that there would be no more problems because of the dispute between the House of Lancaster and the House of York, he married a York family member, Elizabeth, who was the daughter of Edward IV. King Henry VII then united both the red and the white roses into the emblem that would become the House of Tudor, and the war ended in 1485.

Key Figures and Events

To make it easier for you to remember, I have separated the main events and figures that had an important role in the War of the Roses. To start off, here are the main figures of the English Civil War in chronological order of appearance:

- **Henry VI (reigned 1422-1461 and 1470-1471):** The King of England after the end of the Hundred Years' War. Was a member of the Lancaster family and was not very involved in politics. Suffered from severe health problems that led him to leave a certain period away from the throne. Was married to Queen Margaret.
- **Queen Margaret:** Queen Margaret was a French princess who married the king of England after the end of the Hundred Year's War. She was considered ambitious, power-hungry, and greedy, and did all that was in her power to keep the House of York from taking power of the throne in England. She helped her husband gain back power after it was taken by Richard the duke of York. She had one son with the king, who later became king himself.

- **Richard, Duke of York:** Member of the York family, led battles against the House of Lancaster because he believed the government was corrupt and that the king's advisors were being bad influences. Fought several times in wars against the army of the House of Lancaster and was killed in battle. Remained king of England for a short period of time.
- **Edward IV (reign 1461-1470 and 1471-1483):** Son of Richard, the duke of York, gained power in 1471 after defeating the army of the House of York and arriving in London before Queen Margaret claimed the throne in 1461. After this, in 1470, he fought a new battle with the army of the House of York that was assembled by Queen Margaret and lost the throne to King Henry VI, who was given back power. However, in 1471, he took control again of the throne and had the family imprisoned in the Tower of London, where the former King Henry VI died. Had a solid government, investing in trade and making peace with France. Because of his good relationship with France, a deal was made to release Queen Margaret from prison, and she fled back to her country of origin with her son.
- **Richard III (reigned 1483-1485):** After being named protector of Edward V, heir to the throne after King Edward IV, Richard III imprisoned the future king and nephew and took control of the country. He did this under the claim that he was an illegitimate son and, thus, did not deserve to be in power. Although he had control of the country and many allies, when King Edward V and his brother died in prison, his success began to be doubted by the people. He left the throne when he was killed in battle by Henry Tudor's forces.
- **Henry Tudor (King Henry VII, reigned 1485-1409):** Member of the Lancaster family who became

King Henry VII, the first Tudor King. He married Elizabeth from the house of York, Edward IV's daughter, to seal the peace between both families and turned the emblem of the House of Tudor into a blend of the roses for the former Lancaster and York Houses. He was the king who ended the English Civil War and brought peace to the country for some time.

As we will see in the next chapter, where I will talk only about the history of the Tudors, Henry VII's reign was filled with controversy and problems, but that I will save for you to see in a little while. Now let's take a look at a timeline of the main events of the English Civil War.

Main Events of the English Civil War

- **1455:** Battle of St. Albans, where the duke of York first beat the Lancaster army. Is considered the first battle of the War of the Roses. This war gave power of England to the duke because King Henry VI was sick, but he encountered resistance from Queen Margaret and was told to go away from the royal council.
- **1459:** The Battle of Ludford Bridge happened in this year, in which the Yorks were defeated and the Lancasters came back to claim the throne of England with Henry VI as their King. The duke of York goes back to Ireland.
- **1460 (July):** In the Battle of Northampton, the earl of Warwick gathered forces and invaded the south of England to remove King Henry VI from power. Queen Margaret flees the country to Wales.
- **1460 (October):** After Queen Margaret reassembled a new army, they marched to England to remove the duke of York from the throne. The duke was killed and his son, Edward IV, took over power.

- **1461:** Another battle between the House of York and the House of Lancaster, where the Lancaster's were victorious, leading to the rescue of Henry VI. Despite this, King Edward IV was crowned. Henry VI, the queen, and their son escaped to Scotland.
- **1470:** King Henry restored to the throne after yet another battle in the Civil War. King Edward IV goes into exile in France.
- **1471:** Edward IV comes back from France, and in the battles of Barnet and Tewkesbury, the Lancasters were defeated and imprisoned, and King Edward IV took back the power of the country.
- **1483:** Edward IV dies and his son, Edward V, is declared illegitimate by Richard III, who takes control of the throne. Edward V and his brother are murdered in the Tower of London while they were prisoners.
- **1485:** The last battle of the War of the Roses, when Henry Tudor fought Richard III and killed him. Henry Tudor becomes King Henry VII, marries Edward IV's daughter, Elizabeth of York, and restores peace to the country. The English Civil War is finally over.

The Aftermath and Legacy After the Civil War

When the House of Tudor was established, it became one of the most known in England and the center of many changes that happened in the country. As we will see in the next chapter, this included breaking apart from the Catholic Church in Rome and the increase of power of the few nobles that remained. In addition to this, several of the initiatives carried out by the Tudors continue to exist, such as the "Yeomen of the Guard," the oldest military corps in existence today.

The period also brought inspiration to several artists, of

which the most notable was William Shakespeare, who used the Royal Family and the period as base for his work, which is still celebrated today. Even the name of the war, popularly known as the "War of the Roses," was used in several literary works of the time, of which the first was by Sir Walter Scott.

Fun fact: Did you know that the hit series *Game of Thrones* was largely inspired by the War of the Roses, as informed by its author, George R. R. Martin?

As we move on to the next chapter, I want you to keep in mind that the 15th century was a period of transformation for England. We will see the six different rulers of the Tudor dynasty and their impact not only on Europe, but on the world. Read on to learn more about the period and how, from a country composed of Danish farmers, England became one of the most powerful countries worldwide.

CHAPTER 5
THE TUDORS

As you just saw in the previous chapter, the House of Tudors was established by the end of the English Civil War, in 1485. This happened when King Henry VII joined the houses of Lancaster and York by marrying Elizabeth, King Edward the IV's daughter. Throughout time, the changes that happened in England during the reign of the six different monarchs from this house remain as one of the most notable to date. Among the most notable of them was the Reformation, the separation of England from the church in Rome, and the establishment of the Anglican Church.

However, much more happened, and as you will see, most of the dynasty came from Henry VII's family—sons and grandchildren. Although the family existed during a period of creation, the Renaissance in Europe, this did not mean that they did not also go to war. Much changed in the approximate century that the family ruled the country (from 1485-1603), and this is what you will learn in this chapter. Therefore, get comfortable and ready to read about one of the most important periods in English history.

The Tudors in Power

Since King Henry VII came from Wales, we can say that the Tudors were a Welsh-English family who had a deep impact in English history. The most significant of them were cutting the ties of the English Church with the pope in Rome and creating a whole new church based on the beliefs and the convenience, as you will soon see. However, let's take a look at the events in order so that they make sense, and you will understand the importance of each of the events.

Under Henry VII, England became a more unified country and started to expand its commercial agreements. However, one of the main accomplishments of the king was that he was able to build a strong financial reserve in his government, although this did come with exploring the people. During his reign, the government's income almost tripled, making him be perceived as a successful king. He was also seen in favorable eyes by the country's parliament, even though its representatives did not remain in power long enough to make any threats to his government.

He faced some revolts and small battles during his time, with some pretenders trying to say they were direct descendants of Edward V but was able to maintain peace most of the time. His power was also strengthened by the marriages that he arranged for his two daughters, one which he arranged to be married to the Scottish king and the other who married King Louis IX of France. His reign ended in 1509 when he was replaced by his son, Henry VIII, who would become one of England's most important rulers.

Henry VIII

Although Henry VIII was not supposed to be king, he became heir to the throne when his older brother, Arthur, died. He was considered an intelligent and faithful man, who was constantly attending masses and studying languages. Some believe that he was able to speak fluent French, Latin, and Spanish, apart from English, of course, and we loved to read and write books and music. For this reason, he was considered a strong motivator of the arts during the period, most specifically the English Renaissance.

However, his most important contribution to English history was related to the religion to which he was too attached to. At first, he published a book that attacked the protestant reform that was taking place at the time. In the book, he would support the Catholic church, which led him to be seen in favorable eyes by the Pope. However, when his wife, Catherine of Aragon, failed to give him a son that could be the heir to the throne, he did not see this as a problem but instead started a relationship with Anne Boleyn, who was related to one of his previous affairs.

As he saw in this new love the potential to give him a male heir, he started a quest to have his marriage to Catherine annulled. What he claimed was that since Catherine was his deceased brother's wife and that this was against the laws of God, God was punishing him by not giving him a male heir. Therefore, he wanted the Pope to cancel the wedding so that he would be able to marry Anne. This would bring him peace for going against the laws of God, and it would be likely that he would be able to have a male heir to succeed him in power. With his proximity to the Roman Catholic Church, he appealed directly to Pope Clement VII to help him with his quest.

The Pope, although he saw King Henry VIII as an ally for his contributions against the increasing Protestant movement, did not seem to want to do this, and there was a good reason for this. He would be going against what the previous Pope had declared was legal—and that came with a large financial gain to the church. Even though the king had influence with the cardinals and bishops in the Catholic church in England, they still didn't seem to want to support him. They did not want to be left in a bad position with the Pope in Rome just to please the king. Therefore, we can say that King Henry's approach from the beginning had already failed, there was no way that his request would be accepted.

Then came an important figure that would be important in the process, and his name was Thomas Cromwell. He was known as the "earl of Essex" and was one of the king's main advisors who became the archbishop, or the person who made the determination of the church in the country. The earl was an important figure and used the previous abuses of his predecessor, Thomas Wolsey, to convince the parliament that the church should be separate from the government. As a result, several decrees were passed reducing the power of the Pope in the English government, and this was the beginning of the process known as the "Reformation of the English church."

When Parliament granted the king his wish to divorce Catherine and marry Anne Boleyn, it was Cromwell who performed the ceremony. He also declared the previous marriage to Catherine annulled. Suffice it to say that the Pope in Rome was not happy at all with this situation. Losing the power over England meant that it would also be losing political power. As a way to retaliate to the king and the Archbishop, the Pope excommunicated them and finally severed the last ties between both parties.

This was how the Church of England was born, and King Henry VIII, being the supreme leader, was also named head of the church. Although this gave him something similar to a "divine" image to the people, it also brought him problems. Remember when I said that he had written a book attacking Martin Luther, the leader of the Protestant Reformation, and defending the church? Well, people were now wondering what happened to this, since it seemed as if the king was doing exactly this—breaking with the Roman Catholic Church in a similar way that Luther had done.

In addition to this, Henry VIII dissolved most of the Catholic institutions in the country, such as monasteries, and took power over the churches and converted them into what would become the Anglican Church of England, but these were not all of the problems that he faced. You will remember that the reason why he wanted to divorce Catherine was because she wouldn't give him a son. Well, it just so happens that neither could his new wife, Anne Boleyn. As a result of the couples' marriage, another daughter was born, Elizabeth.

Once again, the king was not satisfied and wanted to find another wife, one that would give him a male heir. To do this, with the help of Cromwell, his wife Anne was charged with treason and sentenced to death. She was beheaded, and Henry found yet another wife, his third, who had the name of Jane Seymour. After a few years into the marriage, she finally gave him a son, who later became King Edward VI, heir to the throne, but not all was happiness and joy—his new wife died soon after she gave birth.

Unsettled, King Henry VIII once again found another wife, this time Anne of Cleves. As you might imagine, in such a conservative society, this number of marriages and divorces were not seen positively in the society. What is more, when his marriage to Anne of Cleves ended because, once again, a wife would not give the king another male heir, the Archbishop Cromwell was arrested and executed simply because he approved of the king's adventures. The people were becoming restless, and they were getting tired of Henry VIII's attitudes, especially those where he believed that he could control everyone and everything.

As if four marriages were not enough, he then went on to marry two more times, the first to Katherine Howard, who he ordered to be executed because of adultery, and then to Catherine Parr, who was his last wife and remained with the king until he died. However, despite his efforts, none of the last three wives gave him any children, and thus, Edward was to become king in 1547 after his father's death. His legacy became both positive and negative in English history. While he did begin the process of the English Church Reformation, and his advisor Cromwell helped implement important policies that helped the country, there were also some negative aspects to the story.

First was the devastatingly violent way which he conducted his marriages, either by divorcing the women or having them arrested and killed. Even though he was a very intelligent and impressive king, his attitudes left much to be desired, and there was a division in the country because of religion. Furthermore, during his period of reign, he was constantly in battle with France and with other nations that he wished to conquer and rule. Upon his death, he was replaced by his son Edward VI, who was only nine years old.

Edward VI

Since he was a minor when he took over the throne (only nine years old), King Edward VI, the only male heir to King Henry VIII, reigned under regency rules, which meant that a tutor was appointed to him. It was this tutor, his uncle Edward Seymour, his late mother's cousin, who made most of the decisions for the king. However, this power did not last when

Seymour was overthrown from power by John Dudley, earl of Warwick, who seemed to put Edward in a place of power, but it was just a disguise for him to complete his agenda of power and influence.

Edward, much like his father, was known to love literature and languages and even translated a few books. He was said to be fluent in French, Greek, and Latin. He was also known to be a devotee of Protestantism, following his father's wishes of maintaining the Church of England separated from the Roman Catholic Church. Since he was so young, Edward VI did not have a wife, nor did he produce heirs to the throne. However, when he became sick with tuberculosis, which eventually led to his death, he excluded both his sisters, Mary and Elizabeth, from the line of succession because he was afraid they would go back to Catholicism.

Because of this, on his deathbed, he appointed Lady Jane Grey as the queen of England. Despite her efforts, she remained in power for only nine days before Queen Mary took power. However, since she was a dedicated Protestant woman, this did not please some of the English society, as well as the fact that she was not a direct heir to the throne as Edward's sisters were. Therefore, with support of part of the population, she overthrew the queen and took over power that would be rightfully hers and made several changes to English history.

Queen Mary I

One of the most important things that you should remember about Queen Mary I was that she was the first female ruler not only of the Tudor age, but also in all of England's history—and she made it count. The first thing she did once on the throne was to revert England back to Catholicism, much to the dismay of the country's elite and nobles, as well as Parliament, but she was not happy only to revert the country back to its religion before her father, Henry VIII, but she also was known for persecuting and killing protestants in the country.

During her reign, she had over 300 people killed, thus earning the nickname still popular today of "Bloody Mary." This made the people distrust and dislike her, making her popularity fall compared to when she had the people's support to become queen. In an attempt to make peace with the population, it was suggested that she marry a protestant to bring peace to the country, but as a dedicated Catholic, she decided against it and married the Spanish Prince Philip II in 1554.

As you might imagine, this decision was problematic, since he was not a Protestant but rather a Catholic. In addition to this, she tried to birth an heir with her husband and was unsuccessful—one of the reasons was because Prince Philip was absent from England most of the time, dedicating his time to his native country. During her short five-year reign, she was mostly known for religious persecution and her victims and for not bringing positive outcomes for the English, not even territories in Spain from her marriage. As she became sick, she decided that Elizabeth, her half-sister, would take over the throne after her, thus leading all three of King Henry VIII's to hold the throne at some point in history.

Queen Elizabeth I

Although when Queen Elizabeth took over the throne many people doubted her because of her mother, Anne Boleyn, she proved the people wrong and became one of England's most popular and successful rulers. Contrary to her sister, Mary, she was a devoted Protestant and wanted to bring back the church that her father had previously established for the country. Because of this, she was constantly being threatened, having survived not one but **nine** attacks on her life during her reign, most of which came from Catholic enemies or her Catholic cousin Mary, queen of Scotland.

As a way to appease the Catholics and ensure the Protestants, the queen created a compromise between both religions by reforming the view of the church at the time and finally setting the Church of England. With these changes, most of the people in the country were satisfied and viewed that she had the potential to become a great ruler who would later avoid wars exactly because of these religious issues. On the other hand, a sign of her dedication to religion was that she did not want to get married and resisted the idea when suggested by the nobles, remaining single for her entire reign.

The period during which Queen Elizabeth reigned was so significant to English history that it is usually referred to as the "Elizabethan Age," when England became one of the most important powers in the world. It became known for its maritime explorations, including the discovery of the Americas, by its artistic power, of which the most significant name is William Shakespeare, and the increasing influence in commerce with continental Europe.

The Houses of Stuart and Hannover

After a rule of 45 years, she left the throne to her cousin James since, just like her, none of her half-siblings had produced heirs to the throne. James was the son of Mary of Scots, the cousin who was constantly threatening the former queen, and took over power to become King James I, the first king of the Stuart House who declared himself to be the first king of Great Britain.

During the reign of the House of Stuart, there were six

monarchs of which the last, Queen Anne, was named the queen of Great Britain and Ireland. When the rule of the House of Stuart took place, it was a period of great peace and prosperity for England. Commerce flowed freely because there were no barriers between England and Scotland; for example, and there was an established law that reigned the country. There was no friction between parliament and the monarchy, and the people saw the benefits from the previous incentives made by Queen Elizabeth I, including the taxing benefits for the poorer population.

These, together with the cast amount of natural resources that the country had, led it to flourish and the society to grow. The peace between those of different religions also proved to be fruitful: There were no wars or discussions among the people because of different beliefs. The population was growing and the lack of wars to destabilize the country all proved beneficial factors for the next period of importance in English history.

The line of succession ended with the reign of Queen Anne, who died without heirs, and the throne was then taken by another house, the House of Hannover. This house, made of rulers with German origin, lasted for six monarchs, from 1714 to 1901. It was during this period, that the country suffered its two most significant changes: The Industrial Revolution and the British Empire periods, which we are going to talk about in the next two chapters and explore more of the relationship between the government and its impacts in England as we know today.

However, before we do this, we should go back a little and take a look at the most famous monarchs of the Tudor Era, as you have seen these rulers helped shape England into what it is today and gave the country the peace and stability it needed to prosper in the next centuries. Let's do a small recap and see who they were and the main information regarding each of them.

The Famous Tudor Monarchs

To make your understanding easier, here is a list of all the Tudor monarchs, their period of reign, and the most important information about their period occupying the throne.

- **King Henry VII (reign 1485-1509):** The king who united England after the War of the Roses. He was a Lancaster and married Elizabeth from the House of York and joined the rose symbol of the two houses to create the House of Tudor. His reign finished with a profit in the English financials because of the taxes he charged and at the exploitation of the people.
- **King Henry VIII (reign 1509-1547):** Henry VIII had six wives and was considered to be very intellectual. He spoke several languages, and his most important accomplishment was beginning the English Church Reformation. He did this because he wanted to divorce his first wife who did not give him a male heir. He either divorced or had his other four wives killed until his death, with his last wife, Catherine, remaining by his side until his death.
- **Queen Elizabeth I (reign 1558-1603):** One of England's most famous royals, she did not marry and did not have any heirs to the throne. She ruled for 45 years and was responsible for the establishment of the Church of England. She was considered serious and "married" to her political life. Several accomplishments that would later shape England's

history took place in her reign, which was also known as the "Elizabethan Era."

Tudor Life and Culture

Life during the Tudor Era was short—people were expected to live up to their 35th birthday and that was already a lot. Many children died within the first year of birth and many women suffered miscarriages and died as a result of pregnancy-related issues. Remember, the mother of Queen Edward VI, Jane Seymour, died just 12 days after giving birth to her son. Some people today believe that these deaths occurred because there were little to no sanitary conditions at the time, as we will see in a little bit. After the child was born, a midwife would come and clean the child and change the mother's sheets, although this cannot be fully guaranteed since there were so few documents of the time since women were mostly illiterate. Not knowing how to read or write was one of the things that women were not allowed to do until the reign of Queen Elizabeth.

Until the Elizabethan Era, women had little to no rights, even if they were from a privileged family. While there were some differences between the women who were born poor and did not receive any education and the nobles who were educated, women were not allowed to vote and had to live by the rules established by their husbands. As you might remember, this is a time when William Shakespeare thrived, and although his plays were extremely popular, women could not act. This led men to disguise themselves as women to play the female roles in the theater and in other activities. What is even worse, the women were expected to have one specific and defined role, which was to give their husbands a male heir, something considered essential from what you could see from King Henry VIII's rule. Since the males were the natural heirs to the family's possessions, those who did not have sons were seen as unfit.

During the Tudor era, most of the country was dedicated to agriculture. People were just starting to discover the mining of coal, and that would later lead to the Industrial Revolution, which we will talk about in the next chapter. Because of the limitations in storage of food, most of it was stored in what used to be called "meal chests" where the families would keep their grains and meat so it would last longer. Most of these people lived in small villages, and the cities were not as we know them today—noisy and with crowded streets. The common sounds were of animals, and of course, church bells that eventually rang.

While the customs and traditions were the same for the first five Tudor rulers, when Queen Elizabeth I came to power, things started to change. One of the remarkable things that she did was to provide relief for those who were poor, having been released from slavery a few years prior and taken over the streets as beggars. In addition to this, seeing that the country now had a female leader, the society began to see the importance in having girls learn how to read and write, and thus, in the beginning of the 16th century, they started attending schools with the boys.

In regard to cleanliness, until the toilet was invented during the Tudor Era, people used to answer nature's call in holes in the ground, which you will imagine left the cities with a peculiar smell. In addition to this, with all animals running free, their odor also mixed with those in the city. Finally, to make the mixture more interesting, bathing was not something common, especially among those who had less money and access to running water. On the other hand, the nobles used fragrances inspired by the Egyptians to hide their body smell and be more pleasant-smelling. Furthermore, inspired from the Egyptians, they used a similar honey and dust formula to brush their teeth and prevent toothaches and keep their breath fresh.

Among leisure activities, we could mention some things that are still very common today. These include hunting, archery, and fencing. Of course, we should not forget football, which I already mentioned was created during this time, card games, and an activity that was similar to what we know as bowling today. Other activities also depended on the level of education and money that the person had. While richer folks would play tennis, billiards, checkers, chess, and cards. At the same time, those who had less money to afford equipment would dedicate themselves to swimming, riding horses, and fighting.

As you can see, most of the Tudor life and culture remained the same throughout the reign of the monarchs, with the exception of when Queen Elizabeth I became the ruler. There were not many significant changes during the reign of the Stuart monarchs, even though it was then that the first small steps of what would become the industrial revolution took place. Because of the time of peace, people could focus on improving their methods, and there was also the discovery of the natural goods that the country had.

Fun Facts About the Tudors

- The English Royal Mail was created during the Tudor reign.
- The people used to play games we still have today, such as card games and chess.
- The Tudor aristocracy loved sugar! They liked it so much that they even ate flower petals with it in their meals.

- The origins of football (soccer) are said to have come from the Tudor period, although it was played quite differently at the time.
- Because there was no refrigerator (or even electricity) at the time, the Tudors ate very salty meat, since the seasoning was used as a primary manner to preserve the food.
- There was no fork during the time of the Tudors. However, there were knives and spoons, or people would eat with their hands.
- If you visit some places in England, you will still see some remains of Tudor architecture. Houses with white exterior walls and parts switch wooden planks made up most of the houses, some of which can still be seen today.
- "Britain" was not referred to as such until the reign of Elizabeth I. Prior to this, the kings and queens were only referred to as English rulers. The British name was used to refer, at the time, mainly to the people of Wales.
- You might have heard someone call the flushing toilet "the john." This was because it was invented by Sir John Harrington during the Elizabethan Era. In addition to this, people used to clean themselves with a piece of cloth.
- The Tudors were considered tall for the time they lived in.

CHAPTER 6
THE INDUSTRIAL REVOLUTION

The industrial revolution was one of the most impactful changes that humanity went through in modern times. Previously, only the adoption of agriculture as a form of subsistence can be compared, since it changed from the way people gathered and hunted for food to planting their own crops. The changes started taking place in 1760, with the invention of the spinning wheel to produce textiles, in a device that was known as the "spinning jenny."

In this chapter, we are going to take a look at some of the reasons that made England the best place to host this revolution, why they were important, and how the industrial revolution changed society as it was known. In addition to this, we are going to look at some of the main inventions and innovations that were brought with the mechanization of processes and how society was changed during this period.

The Influential Factors

As I mentioned in the previous chapter, the great time of peace and stability that came with the reign of monarchs after the Elizabethan Period were one of the main drivers that led to this change. This does not mean that the country was not at war—it frequently was. The only difference was that the battles did not take place in their territory, but rather overseas. This meant that the people could live their lives calmly and in peace. In comparison to England, other countries, such as France, for example, were busy fighting in revolutions and dealing with political changes.

In addition to this, there was England's political approach to the merchant market that made it very easy to motivate people to become entrepreneurs and trade. The legislation of the country had changed during the period, and there were advantages for people to create companies and inventions, enforcing the contracts that were signed. One of the major things that the British protected was the intellectual property right of the inventor, and this motivated people to keep on creating.

Finally, we need to speak about the location. England is located on an island, and apart from the sea, there are many rivers that cross the territory. This made it easier for large quantities of product to be transported, both within the country and to other nations. The possibility of transporting the final products in a cheap and fast way also helped the factories see a profit in their sales—the raw material arrived fast from different parts of the world and would be shipped out even faster, ensuring that the production process continued. As the businessmen of the country saw that this was a profitable way to work, they started enhancing the country's transportation infrastructure, investing in modifications, such as canals, that can still be seen today in modern England.

Many of the things that were invented changed society and

helped shape the world into what it became. Technology became one of the most important things at the time and enabled people to increase their production and focus on selling their products to the market, granting the people to earn real money for the first time in the history of the country. Britain had all the possibilities to carry out the revolution: They had the people who would take care of the labor, the natural resources that could be used to increase production, and the land needed to build factories.

The Steps of the Industrial Revolution

One of the main factors that led to the change of production is a previous period which historians usually called the "Agricultural Revolution." As you may remember, since the Anglo-Saxons were established in England, they had a society based in agriculture. People lived and depended on working the land, but they used to focus on growing one specific crop in the same land for long periods of time. This led to the excessive use of the minerals and the nutrients of the soil that would later require the farmers to look for another piece of land to grow in.

However, in 1730, a very clever British man named Charles Townsend discovered a way to make the land produce more by improving farming practices. He developed what is known as "crop rotation," which happens when the land is not used to produce only one product, but rather different kinds of products so that the land does not need to be abandoned. This meant that people did not need to leave their property anymore when they needed to grow, and that their production would increase because of the better use of the land—one year they would grow grains, for example, and in the next, another product, enabling the soil to recover from the previous crop and not be damaged. This discovery was so important that this is a practice that farmers still carry out today!

Now, if you think about the food that was produced, you can understand that when there is more food, people are better fed, and thus, are less prone to die of hunger. Since this was a common problem in the past, when the Agricultural Revolution began, the amount of produced food increased to large volumes, thus giving the population enough to be fed. With this, fewer people died, and the population grew significantly.

Another invention that was essential for this time was the development of a machine that would automatically place seeds into the land. The man who invented this tool was Jethro Tull, who came from a family of farmers, and by observing how people worked, saw that this could be improved. He noticed that the depth of where the seeds were placed depended on each person, and that this impacted the development of the crop. In addition to this, he saw that the process was very slow and thought about ways that could make it faster and less wasteful. Once the seed drill was invented, people saw that there was an increased efficiency in their work, enabling them to focus on other areas of the farm that needed attention.

Finally, you will remember that most of the land belonged to the nobles or to small groups of people, where each person had the right to a strip of land to plant. This all changed at the time of the Agricultural Revolution for one big reason: During this time, the English government signed a law that allowed people to own land. With the best practices of crop rotation implemented, along with the seeding drill, many people saw this as an opportunity to increase their properties, and thus, those who had more money bought land and created large properties with territory that they bought from those who had less money.

However, there was a problem. Where would all these people who now were without land go? Even if they had production, this would not be enough for them to fight with the other producers who produced on a larger scale and more oriented toward the market (a practice that still continues today). Because of this, the people who previously worked on the land were forced into the cities, where they sought jobs and looked for opportunities in what would become the factories that would drive the industrial revolution and change not only the life of the English, but the way the world worked at the time.

The Spinning Jenny

With many people migrating to the cities, there was still the textile industry in which they could work. England, because of its temperature, was an ideal place to herd sheep that would produce wool and other fabrics. However, until the industrial revolution, the process of creating textiles was manual, meaning there was no modernization, and it was done by few separated groups of people dedicated to the activity. People would produce in a slower rhythm, and the process was somewhat demanding, but there was nothing they could do since this was the only way they could survive after their land was bought off by the nobles.

Then, in 1764, another change happened with an invention made by James Hargreaves: The spinning jenny. This was a device that enabled the people to, instead of working manually with individual threads, use up to eight. It is said to have brought a significant increase to the production of textiles in the country. In addition to this, Rickard Arkwright invented what was to become the water-powered water frame, which made the textiles' yarn stronger and more resistant than the spinning jenny, which was created earlier.

Both of these changes led to the creation of textile factories, where the fabrics would be produced on a larger scale. People who were no longer dying of famine, like I mentioned earlier, were able to dedicate themselves to other activities, and inventing ways to improve the production of the country's goods was one of them.

But not all was good. The factory workers lived in precarious conditions because of the lack of management tools for their employees. People were forced to work 12-hour shifts and were physically punished if they did not produce well. In addition to this, they were not safe places—several accidents kept occurring between the heavy machinery and the hot environment. What is even worse, children were sent to work in these factories, especially those who did not have a home or were orphans.

The textile industry was not the only one to have benefitted from the Industrial Revolution. With the invention of steam engines, plow machines, and investments in chemicals, electricity and transportation, the 18th century and the early 19th century were important periods of creation and innovation. Metallurgy was enhanced and coal mining became an important source of income. Read on to find out what some of the main inventions were in those periods and later. Learn how these changes impacted English society.

Famous Inventors and Innovations

Many of the inventions and innovations that took place during the industrial revolution helped shape the next steps that would be taken by great civilizations. Steam-powered energy, for example, was essential in providing power to factories and coal mines. In addition to this, it helped power the steamboats that were later used in explorations and territory conquests. Let's take a further look into some of these amazing creations and the people who invented them.

- **Steam-powered engine:** The first steam engine model was developed by Thomas Newcomen early in the 18th century and was mostly used to pump water. However, an amazing improvement of this system was developed by the Scottish engineer James Watt and his partner, Matthew Boulton. This is considered one of the most important creations of the period. Factories and energy mostly depended on animals, wind, or power obtained from wood. However, once steam power was invented, this gave a whole new use and meaning to the abundant coal that was found in England. With the development of the steam engine, factories were able to increase their production, and transportation was deeply impacted with the creation of steam-powered trains and ships.
- **Locomotive:** Speaking of trains, the first locomotive was invented during the Industrial Revolution by Richard Trevithick in 1804. It changed the way products and people were transported. Even though the invention only came to work roughly 21 years after, in 1825, the concept was quickly adopted by other countries that saw the advantage in the fast transportation it provided. Since they were powered by the coal that was mined in England, the businesspeople saw the opportunity of using a cheap material to provide energy and propel the growth of the sector.
- **Steam engine ships:** As I mentioned earlier, ships already existed at the time of the Industrial Revolution but making them work based on a steam engine made them faster and more efficient. The outcome of this invention was so positive that several canals were built in England to make the goods the ships brought

accessible to the factories that would discharge the raw material and load the finished product for sale. It is estimated that around 1815, Britain already had over 2,000 canals that were built by and invested in by some of the major businesspeople of the time and endorsed by the government.

- **Telegraph:** Although most people believe that Samuel Morse was the sole inventor of the telegraph, this is not true. The system started being developed around 1837 by William Cooke and Charles Wheatsone, who presented and claimed the rights to the first telegraph system. Once it was presented to the public, it became widespread, and companies started using the system to communicate with each other and also with transportation means that need constant information, such as trains and ships. Furthermore, the system would be used in the control of railways and enabled people to know what was going on in the world, which previously would only happen by letter and would take a longer time to arrive.

- **Cement:** Because of the increase in the number of factories being built, as well as the number of houses for the people to live in the city, engineers were looking for a safe way to build houses that would last longer. This led Joseph Aspdin to create a mixture of clay and limestone that would be heated at a high temperature and then grained. Finally, when mixed with other substances, it would harden, leading to the creation of a cement that came to be known as "Portland cement." This invention also led to the creation of concrete, since the only thing to change its composition would be sand and gravel. This invention (which is still used today, although with different compositions), made in 1824,

led to the next great improvement of the industrial revolution: Modern roads.
- **Roads:** If you have ever wondered what the roads were like before the Industrial Revolution, let me tell you; they were bad. Some trips that would be considered of a shorter distance would take weeks just because of the terrible conditions of the roads. That is until a man named John McAdam saw the invention of cement and concrete and thought that this substance could be used to improve the English roads. He created a method in which the road would first be covered in stones, stone dust, and cement, which would make the path easier for people to move in. This led to an improved transportation system and making the week-long trips turn into days, improving the movement of products and people. If you think about how our roads are built today, you will see that there is some resemblance to the process, although cement is no longer used.
- **Spinning mule:** Although the spinning jenny and the water frame were essential to start the work in the factories that produced textiles, it wasn't until Samuel Crompton created the spinning mule in 1775 by combining them both and creating a powerful machine that things really started to change. This is because once the process was automated, different types of yarn were able to be produced: From softer to rougher, making it possible for diverse applications in the clothing industry.

The Impact of the Industrial Revolution on Society and the Economy

You might imagine that once a country that was predominantly agricultural changed into more industrialized methods of production, the society started to change. You are right about this. Apart from having people from the fields move into the city and be part of a labor force that worked in factories and coal mines, this also meant that the social structure of society also changed.

Imagine this: First, there was the king, the nobles, and the lower class, the peasants. Now, England had the monarch, the nobles, the businesspeople, the working people, and the peasants. This is a huge change in society. Because of their increased participation and earning due to the sales of their products, these businesspeople started wanting to have more participation in the highest circles, and this included politics, but it was not an easy feat, since the nobles did not see this emergence of a new wealthy social class with positive eyes, but rather more like a threat.

One of the main thinkers of the time was the Scottish philosopher Adam Smith, who contributed largely to the impression of the new societies with his world-famous book *The Wealth of the Nations*. In it, he talked about politics, economic and social aspects of the relationships between individuals, and even suggested what is known today as capitalism. By his line of reasoning, economic results were made based on the choice of each person or country, who should feel free to negotiate and conduct business with whomever they see fit. This was something that was directly connected to the Industrial Revolution because it was then that people chose what they wanted to do, how they wanted to do it, and that the result of these changes would end poverty.

But even though he became one of the most important and influential thinkers of the time, who we still study today, not everything was quite the way he expected. Women were suffering from having to work at home and in the industry to provide for their families. Children would be sent to factories or coal mines to help with the family income—as the products became more sophisticated, their prices rose, and this led to less economic capacity for the people.

The people were suffering. There was no clean drinking water for the urban homes because the cities had grown too quickly and received too many people at once. Pollution started to grow because of the lack of information on how to properly discard trash. Housing conditions were sufferable, with many people living underneath one roof because they simply could not afford to buy a house. This, together with the lack of safe conditions to work in, led to the creation of a group that resisted the revolution, called the "Luddites."

These groups, which arose in 1811, would protest against the changes in the country and break factory machines. They wanted to take action into their own hands because the government was not doing anything to protect the people, and they were scared of losing their jobs to more modern machines that were being developed. Several factories in different cities were damaged or had their equipment broken, which even led to an extreme political measure to declare these actions as a crime. Although the government tried to reinforce the police to prevent the vandalism attacks, they still continued happening until around 1817.

In parallel to this, labor movements started happening to protect the rights of the people who worked in factories and in coal mines. As I have told you, there were not healthy conditions, especially for the children. With the newly reformed House of Commons in the Parliament, which was adjusted to hear the voice of the people and the business owners as opposed to its previous composition of just nobles and the English elite, new laws began to be studied. Most of the serious conditions that were reported included the unsanitary and unsafe conditions which the laborers faced and the physical challenges and punishments they suffered.

The poor labor conditions led to the creation of what became known as the "Factory Act of 1833," which mainly restricted the work of children in factories and coal mines. According to the bill, those that were between 13-18 could not work for more than 12 hours per day, and those that were aged 9-12 were restricted to a nine-hour shift. Furthermore, employing children in the evening was also considered illegal. Even though the business owners did not like this—children were cheap and productive to keep—they were obliged to follow the law, and they were about to get even unhappier with the labor rights in the country.

Because of Adam Smith's paper, which influenced society saying that the government should interfere as little as possible in the economy, the government feared interfering and creating problems with the businesspeople and halting the country's development. However, the pressure became too much, especially that coming from the influential members in the Parliament, now in the House of Commons. Although there were still businesses represented there, the people made their claims and earned the right for improved conditions, just as the labor union began to grow and become more influential among the workers.

Labor unions started to grow as the conditions of factories and industries deteriorated. Looking after the rights of the people, they fought for healthier and cleaner working conditions and minimum wage to pay for their work. Children were banned completely from the factories and coal mines and redirected to schools. Another victory the unions obtained were working hour restrictions and the possibility of having days for rest and lunch breaks. All of these did not exist prior to their creation and are rights that were earned and remain true still today.

Fun fact: If you like movies and books, you can always read *Oliver Twist,* by Charles Dickens. The story talks about an orphan who lived during the Industrial Revolution and was sent to an orphanage after his mother died. The boy is placed in a workhouse where there is not enough food. In this book, Dickens talks about how the poor were treated during the time and will give you a great idea of how people lived during these periods of transformation in society and the economy.

Finally, we must not conclude our look into the period of the Industrial Revolution before talking about a character that would later impact society. Although he was not English, his ideas were mostly related to the suffering of the working class that was being mistreated. This was Karl Marx. The German philosopher was the man who, together with Friedrich Engels, wrote several articles regarding the increasing differences between the classes because of the Industrial Revolution. Contrary to what the Scottish Adam Smith wrote, Marx believed that the government should interfere in the economy and help those with greater needs.

But what does this have to do with England's history? you might ask. Well, first and foremost, their writing was based on the perception of the English society during the revolution, in which he observed that there was a struggle between the classes, more specifically the workers and the industry owners. They believed, according to the *Communist Manifesto,* that the working parties should overthrow the higher classes and take control of production means, each according to their ability. In addition to this, the authors claim that there should be a shift of private to public property of these factories so that the money is equally divided among the people. Essentially speaking, Marx and Engles write about concepts that mostly go against the thoughts of Smith and his perception of capitalism and the economy.

While there was no action taken on this at the time, it remained as one of the most influential documents, politically and economically, that would later shape some of the events that would take place in the world, such as World War II. Therefore, while I will not mention this in the next chapter, in which we are going to talk about the British Empire and how it expanded across the world, remember it since it will be important for the last chapter of the book, in which we are going to talk about England's place in history.

CHAPTER 7
THE BRITISH EMPIRE

As you have seen in the previous chapters, England was a powerful country. During the industrial revolution, with all the changes that happened in the country, it entered, starting in 1815, a period known as "Britain's Imperial Century." This was because it was when they increased the number of colonies that they had, which amounted to over one-fourth of the world. However, this was just the result of the other two periods in which Britain ruled a part of the globe. These two periods are referred to as the first and the second British empires, when they had power over some other nations, but not to the full extent that they did during what is commonly referred to as the "formal" British empire.

The first empire took place from 1707 to 1783 and was a period when France was their main enemy, as you will remember. It was also a time when the Portuguese and the Spanish were roaming the seas and took over what is known to be Latin America today. At the same time, the British were trying to have more participation in other countries, such as India, where they had great influence and imported textiles and spices. However, this was also a period of loss for the nation, since it was when they lost the British American colonies that they had previously conquered.

In 1783, the second British empire period began with the conquest of Australia and New Zealand. In addition to this, due to the loss of the American colonies, they turned their attention to what is today known to be Canada and were at war with the French for territories in the country. At the same time the British, who were one of the most important players in the slave trade from Africa, suffered a big blow when this practice was forbidden by the Parliament. Because of the Industrial Revolution, the need for workers diminished, and the pressure from society increased to have the practice banned from the island and from all its colonies.

As you can see, during this time, Britain lost some territories but gained others, all of it leading to what would become the period of the great imperial century, which started in 1815. In this period, Britain had the most powerful navy in the world, and no other country wanted to face it—especially after it beat Napoleon's huge and powerful army. In addition to this, with the technology that was invented during the Industrial Revolution, their resources increased, as well as their financial reach. It was a period referred to by many as *Pax Britannica*, from the Latin British 'peace', where there were very few wars and complete control of Britain over a large portion of the world.

The Century of British Domination

Before we start discussing British world domination, it is important that we understand the concept of colonies, which is what they had around the world. Essentially, having a colony meant that the territory would provide the nation that controlled it with raw resources and material that would help increase its wealth. Take, for example, India, which was one of the first of the British colonies. There, they would provide the British with textiles and spices that would be shipped to the country and then manufactured. Once these products were ready, they would be sent back to the colonies to be sold, serving as one of their markets. If you consider the period of the Industrial Revolution, when there was a lot of surplus product and an increase in the production, these colonies served as the perfect place to sell the industrialized goods at a higher price—usually in exchange for gold and precious stones.

Before the British established their period of peace and domination, they had to fight off several countries, which would later mean a strengthened and feared country among most nations. One of their main competitors during the period, as history had already established, was France. The other European country was at the peak of its economy and development and fought hard to keep its territory. One of these examples was during the Napoleonic Wars, when Napoleon was not happy with conquering the territory in Europe, but also those that were colonies, such as Canada. Let's take a look at the events that happened during this time that led to Britain becoming the most powerful nation in the world for more than 100 years.

It all started in 1585, during the Elizabethan Age, when the British went to what is today the United States and established a colony. This was the start of colonization, when Britain developed "the thirteen colonies." The period is known as the "Age of Discovery" because it was when several countries were discovered by the nations exploring the seas, such as Brazil, Portugal, and the Spanish colonies in other Latin American countries. In addition to this, the Dutch were also exploring the seas, as were the French, one of the largest nations of the time.

Apart from the United States, or the "New World," as it was called, the British had established colonies in India through a company named the "East India Company" that also included certain parts of China. The trade between these countries was considered successful, since they provided several raw materials and spices that would be sold in England. In addition to this, over the next years, it also gained territories in what is considered today as Singapore and other Asian countries and some nations in the Caribbean. Although these were claimed to be colonies of Britain, they were majorly investments that were made by private citizens and nobles, who were worried about the expansion of the other countries.

During this time, there was also the advent of slavery, where the nations that controlled most of the colonies would kidnap people from Africa and bring them to their colonies to work for them. This was the case in several countries, and millions of people were transported to these countries to work in agriculture and in mineral exploration. One of the most notable crops of the time was sugar cane, introduced by the Dutch, and that became an important commodity for Europe. In addition to this, the discovery of precious metals, such as gold and silver, in these colonies made them an attractive source of national wealth.

One of the most important laws made at this time was the Navigation Act, signed in 1651, that established that the British colonies could only sell to Britain in British ships. Furthermore, all the products they consumed could only come from Britain, establishing even tighter grasps on the colonies and hindering the chances of other nations to grow their participation in the market. If you remember that I mentioned Adam Smith in the previous chapter, one of the studies that he added to his book was the relationship that countries had with their colonies.

However, even though things seemed to be going well, in 1783, the American colonies became independent, and this was a huge loss for Britain, since they were the largest colony that the empire had. Because of this, they dedicated themselves to the other side of the globe and reinforced the trade they had with India, having even more power in the country and further expanding their influence in the area. One of the most notable conquests of the British Empire during this time was the occupation of the island of Hong Kong, which previously belonged to China and was taken over, resulting in the interruption of trade between both countries.

Finally, in 1858, India became an official British colony after the British had invested a lot of money into modernizing it. This included bringing in materials prevalent from the Industrial Revolution and building railways to connect the country. However, in the same year, the powerful East India Company was closed and no longer acted for the interest of the empire. This was already during the reign of Queen Victoria and in the heart of the Industrial Revolution. By then, the colonies in the far east had been established and kept growing under the British reign.

In the beginning of the 19th century the real expansion took place when the British invaded and conquered a large part of the African countries. For you to have an idea of its extension, most of the west coast of Africa was dominated by the British—from Egypt to South Africa—where they explored the natives for precious stones and metals that would be given to the court to increase the financial power of the crown. At this time, similar to the previous East India Company, the crown established the British East Africa Company, which was responsible for exploring and conquering new territories that would become colonies.

By this time, England owned almost 25% of the world, and some countries were getting restless. As a result, the British parliament gave authorization for some countries to make their own political decisions while under the rule of the British monarch. The first country to have this granted was Canada, later followed by Australia and New Zealand. At the same time, other colonies were starting to fight for their freedom and get away from British rule. This included several wars in African territory that were violently fought off by the British.

However, things would change in the early 1900's when, in 1914, the first World War began and featured the direct involvement of the British. Because of the increasing demands of the war and the attention to the attacks that were happening on British soil, they decided that, for the time being, the colonies could carry out their own administration—there was no time to focus on them with the ongoing war. Little by little, Britain started giving these countries autonomy so they could carry on their affairs while still responding to the Crown.

The situation with the British colonies was to remain the same throughout the first and second World Wars, which we will talk about in the next chapter, and throughout the reign of King George VI and the start of Queen Elizabeth II's time in the throne. During the time, several visits were carried out by the royals to the colonies as they tried to maintain power. The British were no longer considered an empire, but rather a British Commonwealth, which we will learn a little bit more about at the end of this chapter.

Famous Explorers and Leaders of the British

Empire

You might imagine that with all these discoveries and colonization, Britain must have had several leaders to carry it all out. You are correct! Many explorers and leaders were important for the establishment of the British Empire, and we are going to talk about them now. Let's take a look at who they were and what their major accomplishments were.

- **John Cabot:** Italian navigator responsible for the first voyage under England's flag to America. He twice attempted to reach the New World. On the first time, they encountered problems and returned to England. On the second, he and his fleet were successful, although historians are unsure if he reached the same land that was previously discovered by Christopher Columbus or another region in the west of what would become the United States.
- **Sebastian Cabot:** As the name might suggest, he was related to John Cabot; more specifically, he was his son. He was on the first successful trip that John Cabot made to America and was responsible for drawing a map that became famous as England's new territory. Although he was famous for the map, there is another thing that puts him on the list of remarkable explorers of the time: He is believed to have led the first ships to the North of the American continent, where he claims to have seen large pieces of ice (the icebergs). In addition to this, he is believed to have reached a region in the United States near to the coast of the state of Virginia, although this cannot be confirmed by historians since there is no confirmed record of this.
- **John Hawkins:** Although John Hawkins was a famous commander, he was more known for the slave trade that he carried out between the English colonies

during the Elizabethan Age. He was responsible for bringing African natives to the colonies in the Caribbean and what would later become South America. The navigator is known to have done three different "slave voyages" where he distributed the people he captured to the different English, Spanish, and Portuguese colonies. Once he left the slaves in the colonies, he brought back raw material and natural goods that he found in the colonies and sold them for a high profit. It is said that the trips that Hawkins made for the slave trade were among some of the most profitable of all times.

- **William Adams:** Known to be the first British man to travel to Japan, his story is so famous that it even gave origin to the movie starring Tom Cruise "*The Last Samurai.*" According to history, he lost some men and ships during the voyage, and once he reached the island, he decided to settle in the new-found land and even became a military advisor to the Japanese emperor to help improve their military. Along with his second in command, Jan Joosten, he became the first man from the western world to become a samurai and helped establish a trade channel between the English, Dutch, and Japanese.
- **Francis Drake:** This English navigator during the Elizabethan Age became well known for his accomplishments in battle and for being the first man to go around the world. It was with his help that the English army defeated the Spanish, with whom they were in war with for the colonies and their treasures. During his trip around the world, the main objective was to identify potential Spanish colonies and try to obtain from them any riches that he could and establish new trade contacts with these colonies. The

route he followed was eastward, navigating along the border of Africa, then to Asia, reaching the north and south of the Americas, and circling back to England. When he came back from his expedition, once again, he helped fight the Spanish for a few years at sea and defeated the country's navy.

- **John Smith:** If you have ever watched the Disney animated movie *Pocahontas*, you will recognize the name of this English explorer. John Smith was responsible for establishing the first English colony in the United States in the area of what is known today as the state of Virginia. He was captured by the Native Americans, and once there, he was seen as a guest and was well-treated by the tribe until he was rescued and released by Pocahontas. After this happened, he went back to England. He was responsible for the Virginia Company of London's exploration of the area and established a city called "Jamestown." Some years later after his return to England, he returned to the New World to promote English colonization of the area and to motivate English people to establish there.

- **James Cook:** If you remember that I told you how the British traveled to what would later become Australia and New Zealand, you should also know that the navigator responsible for these occupations was a man named James Cook. To some people, he is the most important navigator of the empire who made three different discovery trips. In addition to discovering these two countries, he was also responsible for navigating certain parts of Hawaii, areas that were previously unknown to European countries at the time. One of the most important characteristics of his voyages was that they were very challenging, which granted him several titles with the English court. He

died on his last trip in an encounter with the Hawaiian natives.
- **William Wilberforce:** The only of the men in this list that was not a navigator, he is here for one very important reason: The pressure he put on the British nobles to end the slavery trade. He was a politician who was very influential at the time who believed that the slave trade needed to be abolished, thus he pushed the British Parliament to pass a bill making it illegal to carry out such actions. His efforts were considered to be one of the first humanitarian acts carried out, as he was told by others of the conditions in which the slaves lived, leading him to promote a change. He was responsible for collecting evidence and accounts of the situation and presenting it to the British politicians in 1792, which ultimately led to the abolition of slavery in England and its colonies.
- **Richard Francis Burton:** This English navigator was known for both his expeditions to Africa and Asia as well as his career as a writer. The translation of the famous Middle Eastern tale, *The One Thousand and One Nights*, is credited to him after one of his trips to the region. In another of his notable voyages, he was charged by the British Crown to explore Africa. In addition to this, he was also one of the many captains of the East India Company. Even though he played a great and important part in the colonization period, in his works as an author, he used to criticize colonization and the approach the English people had to it.

The Legacy of the British Empire Today

The British Empire started seeing its decline in the beginning of the 20th century after the two World Wars. After this period, colonies started fighting for independence from the English control. The countries which had already been given independence to control their political affairs remained under a partial British rule. As the number of colonies decreased, and after the empire fell, these countries that remained under the monarchy were referred to the Commonwealth, a name which it still currently carries.

However, the impact of the British dominance of the world brought several important impacts to their culture and to societies in general. One of the main impacts it had in the countries which it conquered was the establishment of a central political government, since these areas were previously ruled by different tribes, each which had control of a portion of land. This demonstration of power and control was important because it helped establish the notion of some of these countries, most notably the United States, of political formats that would later be used to demand independence from British rule.

It was during British dominance that many of these cultures, previously with their own political and legal system, adopted the concept of political serving that was followed by the European country. This included the laws that were passed on by the country, and the financial taxes that needed to be paid. Once they took power over a colony, the British usually assigned a leader that would rule over the country in the name of the Crown and establish its traditions.

In addition to this, it is undeniable that the period of colonization made England an even richer country after the Industrial Revolution. With the high taxes that the colonies had to pay and the goods that were taken from them, they were able to make a lot of money. This included the trade of precious metals and stones, spices, textiles, and other agricultural raw material. Remember that Britain was undergoing the Industrial Revolution, and much of the land that was dedicated to agriculture was being transformed into factories and urban areas since these were more profitable. In addition to the taxes that the British charged from their colonies, there was also the high price that was paid for the industrialized products that came from the island, which leads us to another of the consequences of the British empire, which is the cultural impact on the colonies and on Britain itself.

It is impossible to calculate the effect that the British empire had on many cultures around the world and how these were modified with the arrival of the empire. To begin with, it introduced to several of the countries which it had as a colony its culture, traditions, and religion. It is not uncommon to hear of the efforts made by the conquerors to implement the belief in Christianity with the natives—just look at the example of the Pilgrims in the United States and the impact of the church in Australia, for example. Furthermore, it is important to remember that most of these countries were not at all near the industrialized process that Britain was going through.

The introduction of industrialized goods had a significant impact in many of these countries. One example of this is the importance attributed to precious metals and gems. Before the conquest of the British (and of other empires as well), they were likely not seen by natives to have the monetary value that they had with British society. The colonies' exploration of gold and other goods made them poor while making Britain richer. Still today, we can see the result of these explorations in the jewelry and other items displayed in British museums.

Furthermore, still under the British cultural impact, we can talk about the reflection in several different areas such as in the schools that were built, the architecture that was left, the language some of these countries speak, and the infrastructure that was brought. Some countries were not even near the process of industrialization when the British arrived, and this event changed their view of the world. While some native populations saw their arrival as positive, others fought with certain violence to expel them from the land that was rightfully theirs.

Let's think about a practical example. If you think about the transportation of slaves that the British promoted between Africa and their colonies, this was twice the cultural impact in the colony. First, they would be forced to adopt the British way of life, and next, they would have yet another culture introduced into their lives. This meant that there were not only the changes that were forced by the British colonizers, but also the cultural traditions and beliefs that were introduced by the slaves that were now away from their native countries. This means that many of the countries that were previously colonies had suffered a huge impact on their traditions that could be different today if there had been no external interference from the empire.

Colony Influence in Britain

The same way that there was an impact of British culture into the colonies that it ruled, it is also undeniable that the contrary was also true, in which these colonies influenced British life and customs to a smaller or larger degree. While some of these changes can be seen in the architecture and crafts, such as the Chinese pottery and Indian architecture, there are several other areas in which this influence continues to show today. If you ever go to Britain, you will be surprised to see that it has a diverse cuisine, which was vastly influenced by natives of the colonies who came to England during the time of the empire.

Furthermore, going to Britain is experiencing the blend of cultures at its fullest. There are several natives from former colonies who immigrated to the island to try a better life, and this can be seen in the varieties of traditions, clothes, foods, appearances, and religions that it has. Think about it this way: If Britain was the most powerful nation and one of the richest, it only made sense that people would want to go there and try a better life. Because of this, if you ever visit, you will be able to see this cultural mix at its best, with people from different parts of the world living in the same circles.

Finally, I want to talk about the last item that must be thought of when you consider the impact of the different colonies in British society: The museums. Throughout its history, many of the conquerors were responsible for bringing back to England the objects which they thought were important and of value. This includes precious stones from Africa, gold and silver from the Americas, and much more. Today, when you go to British museums, you can see some of the treasures that previously belonged to other countries and were brought to the island by the colonizers.

CHAPTER 8
MODERN ENGLAND

We have finally arrived at the present. Well, kind of. Before we talk about England today, we still need to take a look into some of the events that took place a little over 100 years ago, since they are essential to understanding some of the things that are happening in England today.

In this final chapter of the book, we are going to look into the England of the past century, its involvement in international political affairs, and how it continues to be an important country with worldwide influence despite no longer being an empire. We are going to talk about the importance of England in pop culture, in sports, economy, and, of course, of the longest reigning monarch of the country, Queen Elizabeth II and the royal family. Join me in this last chapter and see the impact that England continues to have in our modern history.

England in the 20th and 21st Centuries

The decline of the British empire, which we saw in the last chapter, starts in the beginning of the First World War, which was fought mainly in continental Europe. We will start this section of the chapter talking about the changes in the monarchy after we have last mentioned it. In 1917, the house of Windsor came to power, and they have been in charge of the government to present day.

Their reign began with George V, who was the son of Edward VII and Alexandra of Denmark. He was the father of King Edward VIII, who became the king in 1936 but left the throne because he fell in love with a divorced American woman, Wallis Simpson, and the Church of England would not allow them to get married. This changed the course of history, and his brother, George VI took over the throne before the second World War began. The king stayed in power until 1952, when he died, and Elizabeth, his daughter, inherited the throne and became England's longest reigning monarch in history. Her government was highly influenced by the teachings of her father, the advice of her grandmother, Queen Mary, and by her mother, Queen Elizabeth, also popularly known as the "Queen Mother."

The influence of a woman in power of one of the world's most important nations was significant. As you will see in a little bit, Queen Elizabeth II became one of the most influential figures of our time, and her political presence was essential to maintaining England as one of the most relevant countries worldwide. However, before we get deeper into the matter, let's take a look into the participation of Great Britain in the two World Wars as well as the domestic problems it faced in the last century.

England and World War I
England fought in World War I by the Allies (composed by the United States, Russia, Italy, Japan, and France) against the countries that made up the Central Powers (including Austria-Hungary, Germany, and the Ottoman Empire). The

king at the time was George V, who had taken over the throne just four years earlier from his brother. One of the interesting facts about this war was that the king of Germany at the time was closely related to the British king—they were actually cousins!

It was also during the war, in 1917, that to get free from its German-related name of House of the Saxe-Coburg and Gotha, the king changed the name of the royal house to the House of Windsor and excluded all German relatives from being able to potentially inherit the throne. With the remainder of the power that it still had from the British Empire, the British fought along the allies and helped to ensure that the war was won by them.

In 1922, when the war ended, Britain came out as victorious, although there were several problems with its colonies, who were revolting against the British reign. In addition to this, the king was severely sick as a result from battle wounds and from excessive smoking. While he was concerned about the direction politics were going in Europe, he had no strength to fight his sickness and eventually died in 1936, before the second World War started.

England and World War II

In 1939, the world was especially worried with the rise of Hitler and his invasion of other European countries. The United Kingdom was essential in the process of declaring war against Germany since, together with France, they were the first to do so. After the declaration of war from these two countries, others followed. However, so far, the Germans were the only conquerors, but soon, the Italians joined them, and in 1941, declared war against Great Britain as well. It was now the Allies (majorly composed of the United States, Great Britain, China, and the Soviet Union) against the Axis (Italy,

Japan, and Germany), where both military alliances would send soldiers and equipment to fight the war.

Fun fact: Did you know that what was considered the first computer to ever be created was introduced by Alan Turing during World War II to try to decodify the messages that the Nazis sent to their allies?

Great Britain was essential in determining the paths that the war took, especially since they were participating as one of its most important strategists. During this time, the English Prime Minister Winston Churchill played an important role in conducting the conflicts and was considered one of the time's biggest leaders. In addition to this, his cooperation was essential in establishing what became known as the United Nations, which continues to exist today.

By the end of the war, in 1945, Britain had once again claimed an important role in history and became one of the five permanent members of the Security Council of the United Nations, of which the other members include four of the other allies during the war: United States, Russia, China, and France. What would follow is a time of tension which is also known as the "Cold War," but that was mainly between the United States and the former Soviet Union.

England, on the other hand, had other problems. The queen was facing increasing demands from the colonies to be independent. From 1952 until 1997, when the last colony, Hong Kong, was given back to China, Queen Elizabeth II had to deal with the independence of several African countries which were previously part of the Commonwealth and a domestic war in Northern Ireland. The latter no longer wanted to be part of the United Kingdom, especially due to religious differences, and the conflict lasted from 1960 until 1998, when it was declared independent after the Good Friday

Agreement.

During this time, Britain started the talks to join a political and economic alliance with other European countries that would become the European Union. While many of the countries adopted the established currency, the Euro, and agreed to be subject to a common parliament while still maintaining their independence, Great Britain remained with their national currency, the Pound. After many polls carried out with the population, in 2016, it was decided by popular vote that Great Britain was to leave the European Union, of which it was one of the founding members, in a process which was known as "Brexit."

Some of the main reasons for Brexit were the lack of control of borders and immigrant control, which left the British dissatisfied, claiming that they were taking over jobs from the locals. In addition to this, the population and the government were worried about having to comply with the EU rules and standards. Finally, one of the other reasons was the claim that the economy of Britain would be better if they could engage in free market agreements with whomever they desired and that they could apply taxes to other European products that were occupying the British market and hurting the local economy. Brexit was finalized in 2020, and it still remains to be seen what the results were for the British in the long run.

Famous Figures and Events of Modern English History

We could not talk about Britain and leave out some of its most famous figures—both political and in pop culture. While it would be impossible to name all those who were relevant to English history in modern times, here are a few names that you must remember when referring to the country still today.

As you will see, I have divided this section into the most important figures in politics, in pop culture, and then a last section with other relevant figures and events that are part of English history. Read on to learn more about them and understand why they are so important for the story of the country.

Figures in Politics

As you must know by now, Great Britain's politicians have played an essential role in history and continue to do so as history is written. Of course, we could not talk about England and not mention its most important ruler in modern times, Queen Elizabeth II, and how her reign helped shape the government into what it is today. Because of this, she will be the first political figure we speak about before mentioning some other important figures of modern Britain.

Queen Elizabeth II

If you are of a certain age, you might have probably heard about Queen Elizabeth, the former queen of England, who passed in 2022. She inherited the throne from her father when she was 25 years old and is known for having the longest reign in Britain—70 years, which means that she celebrated a Platinum Jubilee. Queen Elizabeth was a notable character in English history since she was in power during most of the 20th century and lived through some of the world's main events—wars, political upsets and downfalls, and modernization.

She was married to Prince Phillip II and had four children: Prince Charles (now King Charles III), Princess Anne, Prince Andrew, and Prince Edward. Apart from the important political role she played in England's history, she was also known for loving her Corgi dogs and horses. She was considered religious (which was reasonable, since she was the head of the Church of England), and her crowning became the first televised event of the Crown. In addition to this, every year she would record a Christmas message to the British talking about what happened in the previous year and giving them hope for the next.

Because of the queen, the British monarchy was seen favorably, and there were doubts about what would happen to the Crown once she passed away. Her family troubles were not only due to the failed marriage between Charles and Diana, but she also faced several allegations against her son Andrew and the marriage of her grandson Harry, Charles' younger son. Due to her importance for the British—and in the world—in the past century, there have been numerous movies, series, and books written about her life and her reign, of which the most currently notable is the fact-based series *The Crown*.

Winston Churchill

Winston Churchill was one of the most famous of the British prime ministers who was an important character during World War II and for future events in the country. He served as prime minister for two times as part of the House of Commons in parliament. He was a member of the Labor party and was considered to have a liberal view of the economy. Throughout his career, Churchill also served the military and as a secretary, chancellor, and minister to the government prior to taking the role of the main politician in the country. Among some of his greatest contributions are his diplomacy techniques, which led to his writing a book on the theme under the name *Diplomacy*. In addition to this, several books and documentaries have been produced on Churchill's life and his importance to the British government.

Margaret Thatcher

Known as "The Iron Lady," Margaret Thatcher was the

first woman to become the prime minister of Great Britain and was also the one that held the office for the longest time in modern times. Her government had both negative and positive impacts, such as the high inflation rates and recession in the British economy, but also enabling thousands of families to have a better economic condition. She was known to have a tough foreign policy (thus the nickname) and not to back out when there was trouble. Because of her policies, she became unpopular with the British and with her own Conservative party, which eventually led to her resigning from the role as prime minister in 1990, but she still remains one of the most influential politicians of modern times.

Tony Blair

Occupying the position of prime minister in 1997, Tony Blair is known for his foreign policies, especially the authorization of military interventions in the Middle East, together with the United States in the War on Terror. He was a member of the Labor Party and occupied the government for 10 years. While in power, he faced public condemnation for sending soldiers to Afghanistan and Iraq and saw his ratings with the public decline severely. Because of the number of dead British soldiers in the war, he was facing public pressure, and the Labor Party eventually convinced him to resign from his post as prime minister in 2007.

King Charles III

After the death of Queen Elizabeth II, her son, Charles, the Prince of Wales, inherited the throne. Although he has worked for many years with charities and with climate change agendas, the most impactful account of him in modern history is his first marriage to Princess Diana of Wales. Together they had two boys, Prince William and Prince Harry, who remain as the throne heirs still today. His matrimony with "Lady Di," as she was known, was one of many controversies and speculations of the public. Eventually, because of the friction between the couple and the fact that Charles reconnected with a former romantic partner, they got a divorce. Charles proceeded to marry this partner, Camilla Parker-Bowles, who has now become the Queen Consort of the British.

England in Pop Culture

We could not talk about England and leave out the important cultural role that it has in the present day. From its general influence by use of the flag in decorations to its contributions to music and cinema, England is still a powerful reference in pop culture worldwide. Although I could name hundreds of personalities that have made an impact in the world that were of English origin, I have separated three of the most significant to tell you about.

Lady Diana Spencer, Princess of Wales

Lady Diana Spencer married Prince Charles of Wales in 1981 and became Princess of Wales. Her marriage to the now King lasted until 1996, when the couple divorced amid several claims of infidelity and discussions. Diana became a beloved character member of the Royal Family, and because of her humanitarian actions, she was nicknamed "Princess of the People," especially because of her work with less privileged children. However, only one year after her divorce, in 1997, during a trip to Paris with her then boyfriend, she was relentlessly chased by paparazzi, which led to an accident and her untimely death. England was devastated, and until today, continues to talk about her influence in the country and how she would influence the paths that her sons took.

The Beatles

Considered one of the most important bands of all times, The Beatles were an English band from the city of Liverpool. Their music became world famous in 1964. The group was composed by four members: John Lennon, Paul McCartney, Ringo Starr, and George Harrison. Among some of their successes were the songs *Let it Be, Lucy in the Sky With Diamonds, A Hard Day's Night*, and *Yellow Submarine*. The band played together for 10 years and were considered to bring a revolution to music at the time. Together, they sold millions of records and earned several awards. After the end of the band, its members pursued solo careers. Today, two of its members are deceased—John Lennon, who was shot to death in 1980 in New York, and George Harrison, who died in 2001. Paul McCartney continues to work as a singer and songwriter, and Ringo Starr also continued his career as a drummer and had launched 20 solo albums by 2019.

James Bond

Agent 007 is one of the most iconic fictional characters in movies, and guess what? He is English! As you can see in all 25 of the movies, he worked at the service of the queen of England. The novels were written by the English author Ian Flemming and have been a huge hit in the movie theaters for his wits and impressive stunts. The James Bond movies have featured several different actors, and even though they are not all based on the novels written by Flemming (who died in 1968), they still show the devotion of the spy to his country.

Sherlock Holmes

Sherlock Holmes has been one of the most important figures in mystery novels of all times. The fictional detective was created by Sir Arthur Conan Doyle in 1887 and used his observation skills to make deductions and solve crimes in England in the late 19th century. The character is known for smoking a pipe and wearing a trenchcoat and a deerstalker cap. He is one of the most known figures in literature, and in London, there is even a museum in Baker Street 221B where a setup was made to mimic the house of the character.

Together with his partner, Dr. John Watson, he solved numerous crimes throughout the 56 published stories, and his phrase, "Elementary, my dear Watson," became one of the most known of all times.

Sports Figures

Apart from being relevant to pop culture, England is also a prominent country in sports, being recognized as the country who created football (or soccer). They have been world champions once, in 1966, when the cup was hosted in their homeland. Football is so popular in England that it hosts one of the most important leagues in the world, also known as the "Premier League." In addition to this, the country has already hosted the Olympic games three times; in 1908, 1948, and 2012, the last in which there were special appearances by the queen, James Bond, and other iconic English characters.

Apart from football, other popular sports in the country are cricket, field hockey, polo, golf, horse racing, and rugby. England is also the home of one of the main tennis championships in the world, Wimbledon, where the game is played on the grass and the players are known to have to wear a white uniform to play. England was also the winner of the Rugby World Cup in 2003 and continues to be an important figure in the sports world, especially those concerning horses.

Fun fact: Did you know that Princess Anne, Elizabeth II's daughter, was the first royal family member to participate in an Olympic game in 1976? Apart from this, she was a participant in several other championships and even won medals in some of them.

David Beckham

For most people, when they think about football and England, the first name that comes to mind is the famous former football player David Beckham. He played in the

English national team in international events such as the World Cup. David Beckham was a player from 1987 to 2013 and played in teams both in England and abroad, including the English Manchester United, the Spanish Real Madrid, and the French Paris Saint-Germain. In his personal life, he is known for marrying Victoria Beckham, who was a member of the famous English girl band Spice Girls, with whom he has four children. He is currently the owner of a football club in the United States where he lives with his family.

Lewis Hamilton (Sir)

This Formula 1 racer and multi champion was born in England and is considered one of the most important English sportsmen of modern times. He was a Formula 1 World Champion seven times, four of which were consecutive. He is considered one of the best drivers of the new generation and has been constantly applauded by the public in his appearances when racing in the country. He was knighted by the queen in 2009, and because of this, his name carries the prefix "Sir" to it.

England Today and Its Place in the World

England, although no longer an empire, still has an important role to play. It is constantly involved in world events such as wars outside their territory and their bans and restrictions on immigrants. The country is one of the largest economic and military powers in Europe and in the world. It continues to play an important part in international and current affairs and is still one of the countries that receives the largest number of immigrants annually, especially from those who were or still are part of the Commonwealth. The increasing number of immigrants arriving to the island has posed a problem for the government, which struggles to provide basic living conditions and fight poverty that is increasing in the country.

In addition to this, you must remember that there has not been, since the early 18th century, a government specific to England, but that it is part of the Great Britain government. Great Britain is currently composed of the countries of Scotland, Wales, Northern Ireland, and England, which is the home of the monarch and of the Parliament. The political system that is implemented today is a constitutional monarchy that has a parliamentary government system. This means that while the sovereign is the monarch in power (who is also the head of the Church of England), they have limited powers and are bound to the rules of the constitution. In addition to this, they do not make any effective decision in the government, but this is rather carried out by the decisions of the parliament, composed of the House of the Lords and the House of the Commons.

However, even though the monarchy has no political power in the country, it remains as one of its most important institutions. Millions of people annually visit England to see where the Royal Family lives and glance at what this country, so famous for its monarchy, looks like. It is safe to say that England occupies a place in popular culture, which can be seen just by how many people attend as bystanders to the events that are carried out in the country—Royal weddings, funerals, and celebrations.

Today, the Royal family and its heirs, King Charles III, William, Prince of Wales, and his wife, Catherine Middleton, Princess of Wales, and their children, are an attraction when concerning fashion and other current events. In addition to this, there is no shortage of media coverage of the family members and the steps they take, with numerous books, documentaries, and series focusing on the royal life and conflicts that happen within the family. It is safe to say, however, that no one really knows what happens within the walls of Buckingham Palace. It is also because of this secrecy and the image that the family maintains that they continue to be one of the most followed and influential personalities in the world.

Finally, I should mention that England has some of the most famous universities and colleges in Europe and in the world. Every year, thousands of students move to the country to study in its prestigious education institutes which include Oxford University, University of Cambridge, the University College of London, and the Imperial College in London, to name a few. Members of the Royal family, as well as politicians and artists, have been students at these universities and colleges, considered among the best and of the highest quality in the world.

As you can see, modern England may not be an empire anymore, but it still is an important country that is worth the visit! Apart from all the history it has in its museums, you can visit castles and other English monuments that are a part of history. If that is not your cup of tea, you can always watch a football match or participate in one of the many public events it holds throughout the year. There is no doubt that once you visit, there will be plenty to do, see, and learn about history and the importance of the country in world history.

CONCLUSIONS

Wow! That was a journey through history, right? What did you think? Did you know about all the information that you read about? I bet that you have learned some new information that you never imagined. I hope this has been fun and that you now feel more comfortable talking about English history with other people.

Throughout your reading, you have learned about the beginning of the Anglo-Saxon culture, who they were and why they were important to English culture. You have also seen that the first English people were direct relatives of the Vikings. Now, isn't that something cool? In addition to this, you have also learned about the Normans and how they influenced British culture and politics. Can you remember the name of the king that took over and unified England? If you said William the Conqueror, you are correct! It was him!

Now, we must not forget about all the wars that England was involved in throughout its history. We have talked about the Hundred Years' War and how it played an important part in establishing England as the country it is today. Do you remember what country they were at war against? Yes! That is right! The Hundred Years' War was against France because of all the troubles that arose when the Normans, who were French, wanted control over England, and England wanted control over the French throne. If you don't remember what I am talking about, you can go back to Chapter 3, where I talked about this and even gave you some fun facts about it!

If battling for 100 years against France was not enough, soon after the war ended, you will remember that England entered its Civil War, also named the 'War of the Roses'. This was a battle between the House of Lancaster and the House of York to see who would become the rightful heirs to the throne after the Normans left power. Well, we all know how that ended—with both houses being unified as one and becoming the House of Tudor, which had some of the most important rules of England.

Remember that it was during the rule of the Tudors that the English Reformation took place, and they cut ties with the church in Rome to create the Church of England. In addition to this, there was a lot of struggle for power and many family issues (don't forget about King Henry VIII's six wives!) that paved the way for the future of England. We learned where the name "Bloody Mary" comes from, and we saw that it was another Elizabeth, the I, that had the second longest reign in England, only after another Elizabeth, the II.

As you read, you have also learned about the industrial revolution and how it was important for England and for other countries with which it had a relationship. On a positive note, there was more food and people lived longer, but their living conditions were not favorable, since many people moved to the city, and it was not prepared for this. There was also the issue of children working in the coal mines and in the factories, something that was not at all okay—at least it was soon banished. Out of all the inventions that I told you about, which one do you like the best? I can say that one of my favorites is the locomotive! I can remember seeing old movies with it releasing the smoke and making its way through the trails.

Next, we also saw the creation of the British empire and the impact that it had on the countries it conquered. We saw how the British arrived in the United States, Australia, New Zealand, and even in Japan! Wow! They were really big—it seems like they were everywhere! And you know, you are not really wrong to think this way because they really were. You have read about the main explorers and leaders of the time as well as the influence that the empire had on many countries today.

Finally, we talked about modern England and its place in the world more recently. We saw the important part it played in world events and how they were even responsible for creating the first computer ever. That, dear reader, is some pretty amazing stuff. And, of course, we could not leave out one of the main attractions of the country today: The Royal Family. As you saw, some people go to England just to try and get a peek of them or visit Buckingham Palace. Even though Queen Elizabeth II is no longer living, she made some pretty important things during her reign. We are now left with what to expect from her heirs and how they will carry out their royal duties.

As I get ready to say my goodbye, I want you to seize the opportunity to take a look into the additional material that I mentioned throughout the book but remember to ask your parents for permission to see if they are age-appropriate for you. There are many movies and books about English history written by English authors that you can watch and learn more from. Maybe you can ask your caretaker to look up some of this information for you or even ask your teacher about it. They certainly will be able to give you more information on more books and movies you can watch that are not violent or inappropriate for your age.

Now, with everything that you learned, I suggest that you consider visiting England at some point in your life or, if you live there, that you have learned some more about the history of this important nation to the world. If you have the opportunity, you should go to one of the museums in London, more specifically the British Museum, where they have several artifacts from the time and some pretty amazing things for you to see. I bet that you would like that; to see what some of the weapons were like and even some of the objects they used. I can assure you that it is really all very fascinating.

As I say my goodbye, I hope that you have enjoyed reading this book and that you found the information fun and entertaining. As I said in the beginning, there is no need to expose yourself to violence or adult content to learn about history. What is even better: It can be fun! Think about all the things that you learned and that you now know because you have read this book. You know about kings and queens, Vikings, sea explorers, inventions, and even why some countries still speak English today. Who knows if some day, when you visit a castle, you will remember what you learned in this book.

I hope you enjoyed it and see you next time!

Note for the parents:

I hope that this book has exceeded your expectations and that by reading it, your child will be able to learn important information about the history of England in a simple and fun way without needing to resort to excessive violence or inappropriate stories. I hope they have enjoyed reading and that the content of this book will help them increase their knowledge about world events related to English history.

REFERENCES

5 amazing facts about the Anglo-Saxons. (2022, September 22). Learning Mole. https://learningmole.com/5-amazing-facts-about-the-anglo-saxons/

Anglo Saxon Kings. (2016, January 12). The Royal Family. https://www.royal.uk/anglo-saxon-kings

Anglo-Saxons: a brief history. (2019). The Historical Association. https://www.history.org.uk/primary/resource/3865/anglo-saxons-a-brief-history

Anglo-Saxons: Facts for kids. (2017, July 6). National Geographic Kids. https://www.natgeokids.com/uk/discover/history/general-history/anglo-saxons/

Barlow, F. (2019). William I - The Battle of Hastings. In *Encyclopædia Britannica*. https://www.britannica.com/biography/William-I-king-of-England/The-Battle-of-Hastings

Barlow, F. (2023). William I - King of England. In *Encyclopædia Britannica*. https://www.britannica.com/biography/William-I-king-of-England/New-alliances

Bayeux Museum. (2019). *Tapisserie de Bayeux* . https://www.bayeuxmuseum.com/en/the-bayeux-tapestry/

Beano. (2023, February 7). *20 interesting fun facts about the Tudor times*. https://www.beano.com/posts/tudor-facts

Beck, E. (2015, March 18). *Agricultural Revolution*. History Crunch. https://www.historycrunch.com/agricultural-revolution.html#/

Beck, E. (2016, January 2). *Labor movement in the Industrial Revolution*. History Crunch. https://www.historycrunch.com/labor-movement-in-the-industrial-revolution.html#/

Beck, E. (2017, June 1). *Why was Britain the first country to Industrialize?* History Crunch. https://www.historycrunch.com/why-was-britain-the-first-country-to-industrialize.html#/

Beyer, G. (2023, March 10). *The Hundred Years' War: England & France's most intense rivalry*. TheCollector. https://www.thecollector.com/hundred-years-war-england-france-rivalry/

Brain, J. (2019). *Timeline of the British Empire*. Historic UK. https://www.historic-uk.com/HistoryUK/HistoryofBritain/Timeline-Of-The-British-Empire/

Brain, J. (2022, May 3). *William the Conqueror*. Historic UK. https://www.historic-

uk.com/HistoryUK/HistoryofEngland/William-The-Conqueror/
Cartwright, M. (n.d.). *Hundred Years' War*. World History.org. Retrieved March 17, 2020, from https://www.worldhistory.org/Hundred_Years'_War/

Cartwright, M. (2019, January 23). *The impact of the Norman conquest of England*. World History Encyclopedia. https://www.worldhistory.org/article/1323/the-impact-of-the-norman-conquest-of-england/

Chandler, G. (2020, June 29). *British Empire facts!* National Geographic Kids. https://www.natgeokids.com/nz/discover/history/general-history/british-empire-facts/

Ellis, S. (2023, April 20). In the wake of the great British explorers. *British Heritage*. https://britishheritage.com/history/in-the-wake-of-the-great-british-explorers

Elton, G. (2019). Henry VIII - The breach with Rome. In *Encyclopædia Britannica*. https://www.britannica.com/biography/Henry-VIII-king-of-England/The-breach-with-Rome

Encyclopaedia Britannica. (2019). *British Empire - Dominance and dominions*. https://www.britannica.com/place/British-Empire/Dominance-and-dominions

Encyclopaedia Britannica. (2020, October 12). *Decline of the British Empire*. https://www.britannica.com/summary/Decline-of-the-British-Empire

Encyclopedia Britannica. (n.d.). *Wars of the Roses - The triumph of Edward IV*. https://www.britannica.com/event/Wars-of-the-Roses/The-triumph-of-Edward-IV

Encyclopedia Britannica. (2018). *Anglo-Saxon | people*. https://www.britannica.com/topic/Anglo-Saxon

Encyclopedia Britannica. (2019). *Hundred Years' War | Summary, Causes, & Effects*. https://www.britannica.com/event/Hundred-Years-War

Fitzgerald, R. D. (2019). *The social impact of the Industrial Revolution*. Encyclopedia.com. https://www.encyclopedia.com/science/encyclopedias-almanacs-transcripts-and-maps/social-impact-industrial-revolution

Foster, J. (2022, June 13). *5 great British explorers*. World of Camping Blog. https://www.worldofcamping.co.uk/blog/newsletters/5-great-british-explorers.html

Fun facts for kids about Anglo-Saxons. (2017, January 4). Easy Science for Kids. https://easyscienceforkids.com/facts-about-anglo-saxons/?utm_content=cmp-true

Greatest British explorers of all time. (n.d.). Pantheon World. https://pantheon.world/profile/occupation/explorer/country/united-kingdom

Hagele, L. (2022, March 24). *Who were the Anglo-Saxons? This is their incredible history.* TheCollector. https://www.thecollector.com/who-were-the-anglo-saxons/

Hales, S. (2022, October 14). *Facts about the Battle of Hastings: 7 things you probably didn't know.* Discover Britain. https://www.discoverbritainmag.com/battle-hastings-facts/

Harrison, J. (2015). Who were the Anglo-Saxons? *The British Library.* https://www.bl.uk/anglo-saxons/articles/who-were-the-anglo-saxons

History.com. (2018, August 21). *Hundred Years' War.* A&E Television Networks. https://www.history.com/topics/middle-ages/hundred-years-war

History.com. (2022, August 10). *Battle of Hastings: Facts, date & William the Conqueror.* https://www.history.com/topics/european-history/battle-of-hastings

Hudson, A. (2020). The Battle of Hastings: fact and fiction. *The British Library.* https://www.bl.uk/anglo-saxons/articles/the-battle-of-hastings-fact-and-fiction

Jackson, B. W. (1957). Britain's Imperial legacy. *Foreign Affairs, 35*(3), 411–421. https://doi.org/10.2307/20031238

James. (2021, December 7). *Famous Anglo-Saxons.* Primary Facts. https://primaryfacts.com/8738/famous-anglo-saxons/?utm_content=cmp-true

Johnson, B. (2019a). *The Norman conquest of England.* Historic UK. https://www.historic-uk.com/HistoryUK/HistoryofEngland/The-Norman-Conquest/

Johnson, B. (2019b). *Wars of the Roses.* Historic UK. https://www.historic-uk.com/HistoryUK/HistoryofEngland/The-Wars-of-the-Roses/

Kings and Queens from 1066. (2018, August 3). The Royal Family. https://www.royal.uk/kings-and-queens-1066

Larson, R. (2018, June 20). *Life in Tudor England (Part One).* Tudor Dynasty. https://tudorsdynasty.com/life-in-tudor-england-part-one/

McFadden, C. (2022, December 2). *34 Industrial Revolution inventions that changed the world forever.* Interesting Engineering. https://interestingengineering.com/innovation/34-industrial-revolution-inventions-that-changed-the-world

Moore Devlin, T. (2021, January 21). *What's the difference between Britain, England and the UK?* Babbel Magazine. https://www.babbel.com/en/magazine/difference-between-britain-england-and-the-uk

Morrill, J. S., & Greenblatt, S. J. (2018). Elizabeth I | Biography, facts, mother, & death. In *Encyclopædia Britannica.*

https://www.britannica.com/biography/Elizabeth-I

National Geographic Kids. (2017, March 4). *10 facts about the Tudors*. https://www.natgeokids.com/uk/discover/history/general-history/tudor-facts/

National Geographic Society. (2022, May 20). *Norman conquest*. National Geographic. https://education.nationalgeographic.org/resource/norman-conquest/

Ollivier, C. (2022, May 27). *6 key figures from the Wars of the Roses*. TheCollector. https://www.thecollector.com/wars-of-the-roses-personalities/

Population of England 2021. (n.d.). UK Population Data. https://populationdata.org.uk/population-of-england/

Rex, R. (2017). *The Tudors and Tudor England in the 16th century*. Historic UK. https://www.historic-uk.com/HistoryUK/HistoryofEngland/The-Tudors/

Smith, P. (2022, December 13). *The British Empire: Pros and cons*. Historic Cornwall. https://www.historic-cornwall.org.uk/the-british-empire-pros-and-cons/

Soaft, L. (2022, March 2). *Tudor history: The complete overview*. TheCollector. https://www.thecollector.com/tudor-history-overview/

Solly, M. (2021, November 8). *What did Tudor England look, smell and sound like?* Smithsonian Magazine. https://www.smithsonianmag.com/smart-news/what-did-tudor-england-look-smell-and-sound-like-180979031/

Students of History. (n.d.). *Why the Industrial Revolution began in England*. https://www.studentsofhistory.com/why-the-industrial-revolution-began-in-england

Taylor, A. (2015, September 8). Map: The rise and fall of the British Empire. *The Washington Post*. https://www.washingtonpost.com/news/worldviews/wp/2015/09/08/map-the-rise-and-fall-of-the-british-empire/

The British Museum. (2017, February 28). *Anglo-Saxon England*. Smarthistory. https://smarthistory.org/anglo-saxon-england/

The Commonwealth. (2017). *United Kingdom*. https://thecommonwealth.org/our-member-countries/united-kingdom

The Great Courses. (2018, October 30). *Legacy of the British Empire*. Wondrium Daily. https://www.wondriumdaily.com/legacy-of-the-british-empire/

The Normans. (2022, January 27). English History. https://englishhistory.net/middle-ages/the-normans/

The Normans - Who were the Normans and what did they do? (2013, November 21). History on the Net.

https://www.historyonthenet.com/the-normans-who-were-the-normans

Top 10 facts about The Anglo-Saxons. (n.d.). Fun Kids. https://www.funkidslive.com/learn/top-10-facts/top-10-facts-about-the-anglo-saxons/

Walker, S. (2020, June 25). *8 interesting facts about the Tudors.* HistoryColored. https://historycolored.com/articles/5005/8-interesting-facts-about-the-tudors/

Wars of the Roses. (2020, June 3). History.com. https://www.history.com/topics/european-history/wars-of-the-roses

What was the legacy of the British Empire? (n.d.). British Empire. https://www.britishempire.me.uk/legacyofempire.html

White, M. (2009). The Industrial Revolution. *The British Library.* https://www.bl.uk/georgian-britain/articles/the-industrial-revolution

Wilder, R. (2019, October 22). *What effect did the Norman conquest have?* ThoughtCo. https://www.thoughtco.com/consequences-of-the-norman-conquest-1221077

Wilkinson, F. (2022, June 2). *Industrial Revolution and technology.* National Geographic. https://education.nationalgeographic.org/resource/industrial-revolution-and-technology/

FREE BONUS FROM HBA: EBOOK BUNDLE

Greetings!

First of all, thank you for reading our books. As fellow passionate readers of History and Mythology, we aim to create the very best books for our readers.

Now, we invite you to join our VIP list. As a welcome gift, we offer the History & Mythology Ebook Bundle below for free. Plus you can be the first to receive new books and exclusives! <u>Remember it's 100% free to join.</u>

Simply scan the QR code to join.

OTHER BOOKS BY HISTORY BROUGHT ALIVE

Available now in Ebook, Paperback, Hardcover, and Audiobook in all regions.

   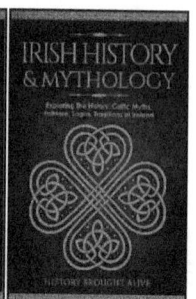

For Kids:

THE HISTORY OF ENGLAND FOR KIDS

We sincerely hope you enjoyed our new book *"The History of England for Kids"*. We would greatly appreciate your feedback with an honest review at the place of purchase.

First and foremost, we are always looking to grow and improve as a team. It is reassuring to hear what works, as well as receive constructive feedback on what should improve. Second, starting out as an unknown author is exceedingly difficult, and Amazon reviews go a long way toward making the journey out of anonymity possible. Please take a few minutes to write an honest review.

Best regards,

History Brought Alive

http://historybroughtalive.com/

www.ingramcontent.com/pod-product-compliance
Lightning Source LLC
Chambersburg PA
CBHW050437010526
44118CB00013B/1572